MINI

THIRTY YEARS ON

Rob Golding

MINI
THIRTY YEARS ON

OSPREY

First published in 1979 by
Osprey Publishing
59 Grosvenor Street, London W1X 9DA
First reprint autumn 1979
Second reprint summer 1980
Second edition published in 1984
First reprint summer 1989
Second reprint summer 1990

British Library Cataloguing in Publication Data
Golding, Rob
    Mini. — 3rd ed.
    1. Morris Mini Minor automobile — History
    I. Title
    629.2′222   TL215.M615

ISBN 0850-459-257

Editor Tim Parker

Filmset and printed in England by BAS Printers Limited,
Over Wallop, Hampshire

Contents

Acknowledgements

The affection for the Mini is colossal. Throughout the time this book was being researched hundreds of people went to unimaginable trouble to contribute ideas, facts, memories and photographs.

Some willingly gave up several days; others turned over complete photo albums without a second thought.

And at Austin Rover, several very busy men who control the success of the forthcoming models took up valuable time to look back rather than forward.

I wish them well and thank them and everyone else who contributed.

Tony Spalding and Tim Parker devised the idea of this book before involving me, my wife Shirley gave it her blessing. Ian Elliott, Mike Kennedy, Denis Chick and Norman Childs provided company research material, and Ian proved that there was more in his head than exists anywhere on paper. His help was invaluable.

Photographs Nick Akers, Cyril Comley and Peter Filby helped with specific problems, while scores of pictures came to light where the photographer is no longer known. Thanks to all those anonymous helpers.

The late Laurence Pomeroy and Peter Browning wrote respectively *The Mini Story* and *The Works Minis*, which are excellent references, while Graham Robson and John Stanton were responsible for much original magazine work. Dave Orchard has the most impressive set of amateur records imaginable.

Most important are those people who made and moulded Mini history and scores gave me help. There were long interviews with Sir Alec Issigonis, Charles Griffin, John Cooper, John Rhodes, John Hanley, Colin Daniels, Tom French, Iain Mills, Albert Green, Henry Coldham, Richard Longman, Lindsay Campbell, Gordon Sked, Martin Peach and Rod Kirkpatrick. Many more sat patiently on the end of a telephone to answer queries.

My engineer brother Mike, and friend and colleague Brian Grice tackled the chore of copy reading.

6

Preface

The Mini was created by the inspiration of one man with as fluid an imagination as Leonardo da Vinci.

For a year, the little car hovered on the brink of disaster. But it slowly gathered momentum to sweep all before it on its rise to race and rally champion, and created in its wake a new breed of heroes.

Because so many people wanted to associate with its success, it spawned a whole industry of accessory makers and tuning specialists.

It even came to the attention of the Rolls-Royce coachbuilders like Hooper and Wood and Pickett, who reclothed it and sold it for as much as £20,000.

More than five million Minis have been built by the company, but it is only in the last couple of years that the car made a profit.

The simplicity of the transverse engine with front wheel drive made it suitable as the power pack for all sorts of glass-fibre sports car specials, like the pretty Unipower.

In thirty years, the Mini has passed more milestones than any other car.

Author's note
During the Mini's thirty year life, the company manufacturing it has been through a variety of administrative changes. So it is true to say that the car has been built by Austin, Morris, BMC, British Leyland, Leyland Cars, BL, BL Cars, Austin Morris, Austin Rover and the Rover Group.

Where relevant, the administration current at the particular period under discussion has been given the name then applicable. This may explain the apparent inconsistencies in referring to what can broadly be described as 'management'.

Foreword

The first Min I had was Minnie Bannister, the world-famous poker-player. 'Give her a good poker and she'll play any tune you like.' (The Goon Show Number 102, Fifth Series, Number Three. Transmitted Tuesday 12 October 1954, 8.30 Home Service.)

Looking back over those Goon scripts, there are one or two lines that might have been tailor-made for the Min that was to come. Like this;

'Hurry Min, every day is precious,' (H. Crun), or this; 'Stop it Min, you're driving me into a frenzy of evil dancing.'

Or this one, 'It's clear, Min—it sounds real cool. Get your woollen crash helmet on—I'm taking it out on the trial run.'

Like Spike Milligan's Minnie Bannister, the BMC Mini is a small memory worth hanging on to.

For anyone between twenty-five and forty-five, the Mini was part of growing up. Look at me. I had lots of them.

Alec Issigonis, who designed the little car, was as clever as Inspector Clouseau. He had a suspicion that all the best things in life came in little boxes.

For thousands of us who had to get around London quickly, the arrival of the Mini was like the answer to a prayer.

The first one of mine that was specially ordered came from H. R. Owen. We stuck wickerwork on the side, rushed it up to Oxford Circus and caned it down Park Lane.

And I had one with a big opening door at the back so that Harry Secombe could come along.

It does not seem twenty years since those exciting days when the Mini created a new era.

It gave mobility to millions and bankrupted textile mills by leading the way to mini-skirts (sigh).

A commemorative book is long overdue.

Signed Peter Sellers
June 1979

1 Issigonis—man behind the Mini

'The most pleasing thing that has happened to me was my appointment to the Royal Society. I think I felt that too many fellows were academic and that an odd ironmonger like me would help redress the balance.'

For Sir Alec Issigonis to admit pride at association with pure scientists was like an agnostic taking communion. He spent a lifetime decrying the value of pure disciplines like mathematics — 'the enemy of every truly creative man'.

Perhaps this was just a defence mechanism. He was, after all, a maths flunk at school even though he was then showing great talent as a designer and draughtsman. He had tried three times at Battersea Technical College to matriculate, and three times he failed in maths. 'I hated it, could not see the point of it and never found any use for it.' Eventually the college principal saw his potential and gave Issigonis another chance to pass his exam and qualify for his diploma. Issigonis swears to this day that he failed the retake as well, but he was, nevertheless, awarded a mark sufficiently high to give him the paper.

Sir Alec was determined to become an engineer.

Issigonis, who died in 1988, was British born in Smyrna (now Izmir) in 1906 to a Bavarian mother and in line to inherit the family boiler-making factory. It was the largest of its kind in that part of Asia Minor and stood sometimes on Greek soil and sometimes on Turkish, depending who was winning at the time. Not far away, on the same island, was born shipping magnate-to-be Aristotle Onassis.

The business was a personal success for Issigonis's grandfather, whose son was also an engineer, but a playboy too until middle age, and little interested in business. When only twenty he was sent to England to study but instead found many diversions. He stayed so long that he chose to confirm the affinity he found with this foreign country and became

Lord Snowdon, who did as much as anyone to make the Mini fashionable, renewed his friendship with Sir Alec Issigonis at the 1978 International Motor Show in Birmingham

naturalized. Only when he tired did he return to run the business. Soon after his return he found among the colony of expatriates in Smyrna Hulda, the nineteen-year-old daughter of a wealthy Bavarian brewer whom he married when he himself was thirty-five.

Issigonis spent his formative years under house arrest and a 'prisoner' of the Germans during World War 1. His father had refused to turn his factory over to the repair of the German Mediterranean submarine fleet and it was subsequently confiscated. However, he did have a maternal aunt who had the good fortune to be married to an Italian and she was able to spread a thin mantle of political immunity over the whole family.

All Issigonis can recall of the hostilities is a regular morning visit from a British Farman biplane based on one of the neighbouring Aegean islands. The crew could plainly be seen manhandling one bomb over the side of the cockpit, but never scoring higher than a goat or a donkey.

When the war ended Lloyd George gave as compensation to Greece the Smyrna strip of the coast, although when Turkey sought to reacquire

its former territory by force, Lloyd George did nothing more than send in
the navy to lift the British nationals to safety. The Issigonis family was
roused in the night and told to take only blankets with them. Finally they
were landed at Malta, where they lived as refugees for six months while
Issigonis's father fell ill and grew weak. Government compensation
gradually arrived and allowed many of the exiles to return to their homes
to pick up the shreds of their lives. The tented village in Malta
dispersed — but for the Issigonis family. In desperation, Issigonis's
mother decided to leave her husband in a nursing home while she
escorted her son to England.

He was fifteen and had never been to school, having only shared
private tutors with the rest of the English community in Smyrna. She
knew that if the young man was to make anything of his life, he needed an
English education. She knew equally well that Oundle School — for
which he had been booked — was now out of the question for financial
reasons. Battersea Tech. filled the gap, and it gave him a three-year
grounding in the basic essentials of his future trade. What he was unable
to learn from the textbooks he seemed to know instinctively when it came
to putting into being his own original thought.

Before taking up his first job, he did the statutory 'grand tour' of

Europe with his mother in a Singer 10. Issigonis had regularly attended meetings of the Institution of Vehicle Engineers whilst at Battersea, and, when he wanted a job, his first stop was with Brian Robins, the Secretary of the Institution. Robins pulled out a card from an index marked 'vacancies' and launched the young Issigonis into the motor trade.

A man past thirty rarely shows brilliance in his work—or so they say. Issigonis was to spend forty years heaping scorn on that tradition.

Issigonis was always arrogant in his engineering. He had scant regard for the allied disciplines of styling and market research and never considered either necessary in creating a new vehicle capable of making or breaking the fortunes of a car company. He delighted in referring to market research as 'bunk'. Once when asked by the Italian stylist Giovanni (Pinin) Farina—who was obviously impressed by the lines of the prototype Mini—if he too was a stylist, Issigonis replied tartly that he found the question offensive. 'I am an engineer,' he said, as if that explained everything. Issigonis was not only arrogant about the superiority of his discipline. He was also selfishly determined that what was right for him was right for the rest of the world. The whole charm of the Mini is that it is one man's package, which has not had its character eroded by compromise and committee decisions.

Issigonis argued throughout his active career that a new car project could quite safely be entrusted to one man. If that man is a practical man, he says, the product will be practical. Happily, he operated in an era when practicality rather than legislation and consumerism controlled car design. When he was designing the Mini, he was able to ignore the need to provide for a radio mounting space—because he did not like radios;

Alec Issigonis with his creation at Longbridge in 1965. The white car is the first production car, built single-handed by Albert Green. The other is a little-changed 1965 specification Mini

Miriage wheels
by invisible means

A. Issigonis

12/3/67

similarly he was able to ignore the need to provide for seat-belts — because he did not wear them. A classic case of his stubbornness arose during the design of 9X — the Issigonis Mini of 1968 designed to replace the Issigonis Mini of 1958. An engineer reminded him that Swiss legislation required all cars to be imported to that country to be capable of being fitted with snow chains. The 9X was not. Issigonis merely retorted that because his car was front-wheel drive, its performance on snow and ice was adequate, and he continued to ignore the need for that extra wheel-arch clearance.

Perhaps because of his penniless youth, Issigonis was infatuated with the idea of making the most of the least. He was never interested in the lavish or magnificent. A story is told that when he was forced to visit Niagara Falls, he preferred to stay in the car and read while his friends made the final stage of the journey on foot. When his full-time service with BMC ended, he chose to comfort himself in his retirement with nothing more elaborate than a Mini and a bungalow whose main attribute was seclusion, within a mile of Birmingham's centre.

Issigonis's first job in 1928 was in a London design office run by one Edward Gillett, who wanted to devise an automatic clutch release incorporated in the gear-stick. Issigonis was both draughtsman (the only one) and salesman, and he spent five fairly fruitless years trying to get it

Most good ideas are first mapped out on the back of an envelope. Issigonis planned his hydraulic transmission on the front of one. The dream of wheel motors collapsed in a torrent of unacceptable noise

adopted by the industry. Notable amongst those few companies which showed interest was Humber, then recently acquired by the Rootes brothers. Engineering head T. Wishart thought the idea might be of use, but was really more interested in having Issigonis on his design team. Issigonis complied. The semi-automatic idea had reached the stage of patents being taken out by Chrysler, but General Motors had, almost simultaneously, devised synchromesh, and this development convinced Issigonis he was wasting his time. Also at Humber, he found himself working with protagonists of independent suspension, who were soldiering down the path of innovation even though parts of the British industry were convinced that improved road surfaces would make the refinement unnecessary.

At this stage, Issigonis was living with his mother in Kenilworth in a rented house. The garage was strewn with pieces of an Austin Seven Ulster, which was first heavily adapted to make it competitive at the nearby Shelsley Walsh hillclimb, then cannibalized to create the famous Issigonis Lightweight Special. This car not only boasted independent suspension and rubber springing but also—eventually—proved quite by chance that negative camber is an essential prerequisite of good traction. That lesson was learned after the war when, at a meeting in 1949, a couple of rings of rubber spring were removed from the rear suspension and times improved dramatically.

In 1936—three years before the Lightweight Special first raced— Issigonis moved to work for Britain's biggest motor manufacturer, Morris, at Cowley. Under the direction of Leonard Lord, Morris was going through an 'American phase'. Chief engineer Robert Boyle suggested imitating the transatlantic engineering style of doing everything separately—engine, gearbox, suspension, chassis and back axle were all to be developed by independent teams. Issigonis was recruited for the back axle, even though his nature told him that decentralization on this scale was very wrong. Although he was nominated for the rump task, he convinced Boyle that his experience in suspensions should be exploited. The hapless suspensions man was awarded the back axle.

The departmental scheme did not last long, for Leonard Lord argued with the Morris founder, Lord Nuffield, and retired—only to join the rival Austin the following year. Boyle went back to Morris Engines at Coventry and his suggested administration was disbanded. Issigonis stayed on to develop suspensions even though the management wanted to persevere with beam axles, as shown by the 1939 Series M Morris Ten. 'Coil spring and wishbone' independent suspension was due to be launched on a car timed for the 1939 Motor Show, but the war intervened and the system did not reach the public until 1947, when the MG YA $1\frac{1}{4}$- litre saloon was introduced. A refinement of the design persists with the MGB sports car.

During the war, Issigonis was kept fully employed making prototype military equipment. One project that lasted longer than the rest was a motorized luggage-carrier capable of being dropped, in kit form, by parachute. When war ended, the sigh of relief that went up throughout

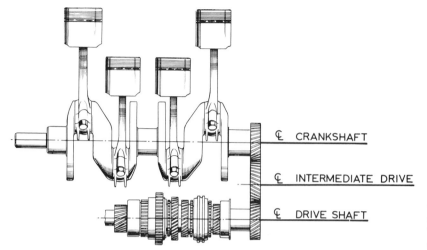

Left A simplified plan drawing of how the Mini crankshaft transmits power to the road wheels

CRANKSHAFT

INTERMEDIATE DRIVE

DRIVE SHAFT

Below At the time the Mini power unit was considered complex. This Theo Page drawing of 1959 shows why. Today, nobody thinks twice about it

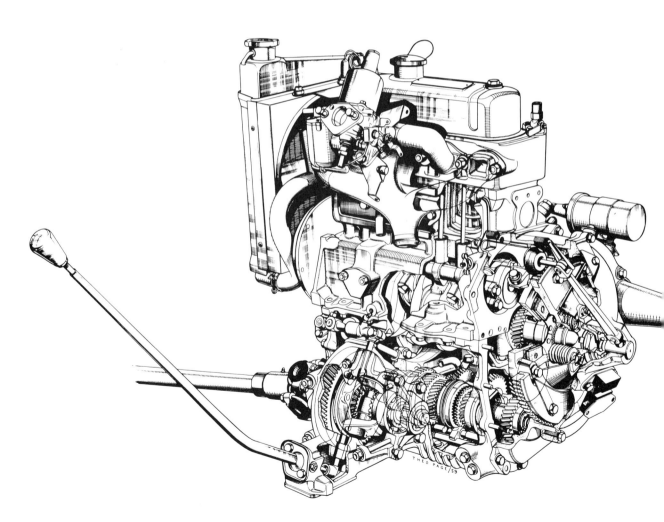

Theo Page's second drawing of the first Mini shows a left-hand drive car

Europe was construed by many motor companies as the sign for the end of austerity. They planned large cars. Issigonis, however, was still thinking small and he convinced the Morris management to think small with him, and entrust him with a compact design team to put ideas on paper. What he had in mind was a small four-seater which had sophisticated handling and would be cheap to run. What he did not know at that stage was that his tentative ideas were to give birth to the first British car to sell a million—the Morris Minor, forerunner of the Mini.

One night in 1948, Issigonis instructed the mechanics in his design team to slice one of the precious pre-production prototypes of the Morris Minor from bumper to bumper. The two halves were moved outwards until the 'Greek' in Issigonis surfaced and reached a decision. Four extra inches in the width had made all the difference. The American influence in the V-shaped split windscreen and the bulbous bonnet and wings were not necessarily pretty, for the last thing Issigonis would allow the car to be described as was stylish. But he was now certain that it was elegant and, above all, well proportioned. His ability to recognize it he puts down to his early exposure to the architectural treasures of his birthplace.

Issigonis had several ambitions for the car which were frustrated because of the speed with which it had to be produced. It was ready for October 1948 and boasted integral body construction, torsion-bar front suspension, rack-and-pinion steering, and fourteen-inch wheels instead of the standard fifteen or sixteen. They did not produce the harshness in

Left The full-size XC 9001 was the project which eventually gave rise to the 1800. Although it was the first to get Issigonis's attention after his return to Longbridge, it had to wait until after the Mini and the 1100 to be made. At this stage it was rear-wheel drive with central springing using water as the medium. The ride was harsh, the handling remarkable

Opposite, below The rear view

XC 9002 was 1100 size and the first stage in down-sizing, seen here as a scale model compared with a Morris Minor

Left At last. XC 9003 was the right size, although styling detail at the front was to change

Opposite Existing Austin grilles were used as camouflage for the running prototypes, nick-named Orange Boxes

Left At the back there were even more changes necessary

Opposite Production Minis lost the easy engine access of this Orange Box and there were to be many other changes from the specification which is obvious here

Opposite Early Mini. In fact, a 1962 Super de-luxe with 'handlebars' on the bumpers

Right The original production car engine installation. Compare this shot with the earlier one of the Orange Box engine

Replacement Mini? Issigonis's 9X prototype of 1968 was eventually abandoned

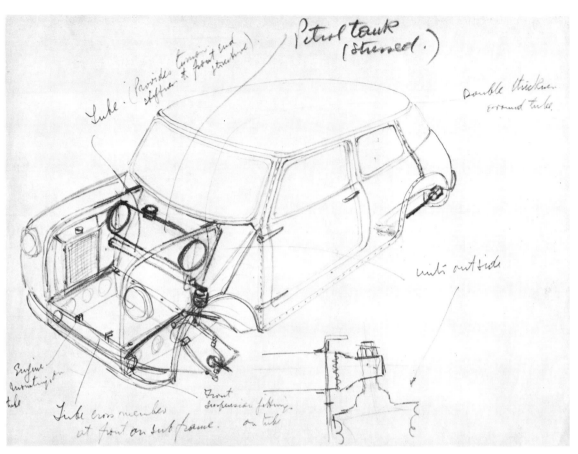

Petrol tank (stressed.)

Tube. (Provides torsional and stiffness & front end structure.)

Double thickness around tube

cuts outside

Engine mounting on tube

Tube cross members at front on sub frame.

Front suspension fitting on tube.

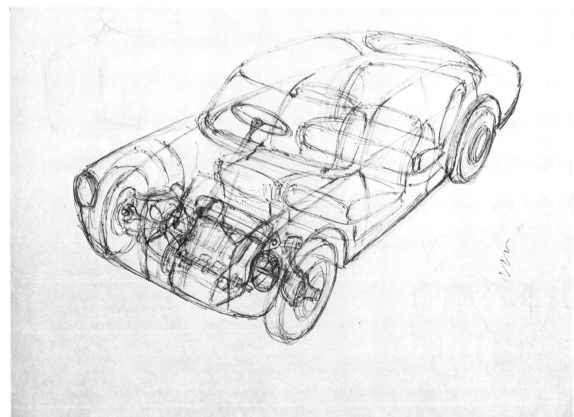

These three drawings by
Issigonis illustrate his simple
style which is both imaginative
and entertaining

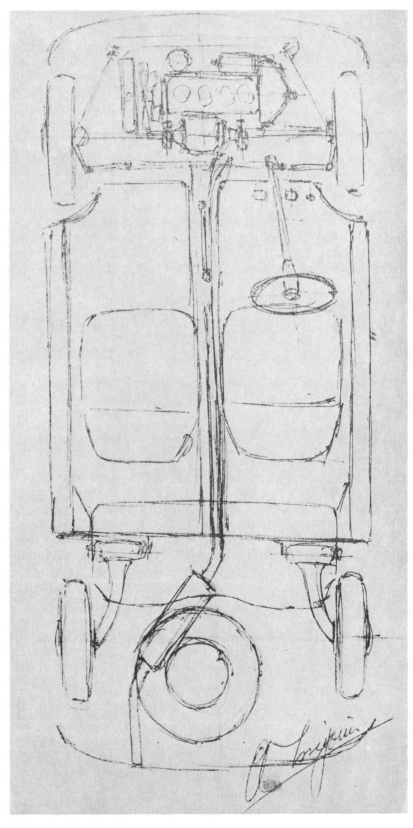

ride expected of them and had the advantage (which was not then fully appreciated) of decreasing the unsprung weight. In prototype form (when code-named Mosquito) it had carried a flat-four engine, an independently sprung rear end and front-wheel drive, but he did not have the time to add these three refinements. It was the first car to have headlamps incorporated in the front grille—a feature which changed when American regulations set what was expected to become a worldwide standard height for headlamps. The Press hailed the car as setting new standards of road-holding for a family car.

In 1952, Morris merged with Austin. Issigonis accepted the inevitable rationalization of engines which killed his hopes for the flat-four, and substituted the lighter and more powerful 803 cc overhead-valve Austin engine for the 918 cc side-valve Series E engine which had been inherited from the Morris Eight. Issigonis tired of the company politics, which were the natural consequence of merger, and accepted an invitation from Alvis to take a clean sheet of paper and design a sports saloon from scratch. The $3\frac{1}{2}$-litre aluminium V8-engined car produced was new from stem to stern and capable of more than 110 mph. It had a four-speed box with only two gears, electric overdrive on both, and rubber suspension. However, Alvis decided that it could not afford the expense of tooling for such an adventurous proposition, and scrapped the car and all the drawings for it. The Issigonis sports saloon was not in the Alvis idiom of the day, and it was also a good deal more expensive than had been intended. Management had conflicting demands for investment cash and the decision went against the new car. Instead, the investment was made in a new fourteen-cylinder engine known as the Leonides, which powered the S55 Westland Whirlwind helicopter. The abortive work cost Issigonis three years, but gave him invaluable design experience.

As a result, in 1956 he went to the BMC design headquarters at Longbridge, Birmingham, at the invitation of Leonard Lord. There he found that the project he had abandoned when he joined Alvis had been put through its paces with extremely satisfactory results. It was the front-wheel-drive Minor, registration number TFC 717. Despite the obvious enthusiasm that existed for this configuration—contrived through a drive arrangement later used by Fiat for the 128—the immediate preoccupation was a rear-wheel-drive 1500 cc car which later turned into the front-drive 1800 series.

The Suez crisis broke in September of that year, when Nasser, the Egyptian dictator, cut the oil pipeline feeding the West. In so doing he had triggered the most brilliant idea in automotive history.

2 Conception, birth and manufacture

Leonard Lord, the company chairman, was nothing if not a purist, so the rash of bubble cars that appeared in response to the post-Suez petrol rationing offended him. He dearly wanted to clear them from the streets and substitute a small, capable car with big-car performance. Clearly, he now had the man to do it.

Issigonis was told to drop everything and produce a miniature of the Minor with the minimum of material surrounding the maximum amount of space. Issigonis gathered around him eight people; the most important were Jack Daniels, who shared Issigonis's enthusiasm for suspension systems; Chris Kingham, the engine man who had been with him on the Alvis project; and Charles Griffin from Cowley. The other men who lost a lot of sleep during the crash development programme were John Sheppard and Vic Everton in the body-jig shop; Ron Dovey, who built the bodies; Dick Gallimore, who laid out the experimental bodies; and George Cooper, the only member of the team at Cowley whose job was to check the layouts. It was a close-knit team which had an uncanny knack of instant understanding, and this was fuelled by the system of communication that Issigonis had devised. He discovered in himself the ability to freehand sketch, in precise detail, the ideas he had in mind. The fact that he was not a fully qualified engineer did not matter. The engineering assistants could translate his freehand sketches into technical blueprints. What did matter was that the Leonardo da Vinci-style meanderings were practical. He often used sketches instead of words as memos to himself, and although he liked to describe himself as an ironmonger, there was no doubt that Issigonis could have been a convincing artist, had he wished. His work suggested it and his appearance confirmed it. Hawk-faced and sensitive-looking with a stooped stance, long fingers and expansive gestures, he is Everyman's image of an eccentric artist.

It was March 1957 when Leonard Lord took the courageous decision to shelve the other projects he had in hand and to commission the

miniature. With the intention of cashing-in on an artificial problem when motorists were rationed to less than ten gallons of petrol a month, the urgency was considerable. Issigonis set about his task from the point of view of an occupant—one of four occupants—of the car he had in mind. He calculated that without allowing for engine space or luggage bay, the car needed to be at least 8 feet 9 inches long, 4 feet 2 inches wide and 4 feet 4 inches high.

At the time the work was being carried out, BMC was going through a phase of naming cars after places—Westminster, Cambridge, and so on. When his colleagues saw that the new car was to aim at a 'new market sector' they began to refer to it as the Austin Newmarket.

Issigonis had already decided in his own mind that it would be front-wheel drive—thus doing away with the transmission tunnel. A shallow tunnel was designed into the car, however, to make sure of a six-inch ground clearance for the exhaust system. There was nothing particularly startling about his decision to place the engine transversely, for there were plenty of precedents for mounting the crankshaft across the car. The more critical decision was the siting of the gearbox. If he had settled for a two-cylinder unit, he could have managed to fit the box in line with the crankcase. But with a four-cylinder unit—which was virtually essential to get the performance and refinement he was after—an in-line gearbox would have restricted the steering lock unacceptably. He turned his mind to the generally unused area beneath the engine between the

Above Albert Green—single-handed builder of the first production Mini
Below The first milestone came up after three years—12 December 1962.

Above Water testing became an unpleasant essential in the first few months of production

Below The Mini sub-frame was conceptually a brilliant piece of design, but in use it has become well known for its ability to rust, particularly at the rear. This is the very latest six-point mounted design.

wheels. Commonsense said that it would work. The only deterrent was
that it had not been done before.

Accepting the challenge was typical of Issigonis. If logic dictated
something could be done, he was not frightened by the unspoken
question: 'Then why hasn't it been done before?' If he was wrong, and it
was found that engine and gearbox would not run on the same sump oil,
the timing of the new car project would collapse and BMC's already
failing competitiveness in world markets would be shattered. As it was,
there was little more than six months' development time available to
build and run a prototype. In July 1958, Leonard Lord took a five-minute
drive around the Longbridge site, and without any visible reservations
told Issigonis to have it in production within twelve months. That was
only fifteen months after the design team had started work, and nine
months since the first prototype had gone on the road.

The small wheels were as logical a choice to Issigonis as the transverse
engine. The objection to ten-inch rims was that they could only carry
small tyres, which were incapable of ridding the car of the harshness of a
rough road. Issigonis, however, was confident that his suspension system
would provide the foil. His colleague of previous projects, Alex Moulton,
was already working on rubber springing. Rubber was seen as the only
cheap solution to the problem of greatly varying total weight. In a car
weighing only about 1300 pounds, four occupants instead of one added
more than thirty per cent to the laden weight. Springs which stiffened
themselves as the load increased were essential, and rubber has exactly
that quality.

15 Successful Years
of the MINI 1959 - 1974

Fifteen years passed and export to Canada was in full swing. The Heath Robinson design for the raised bumper line indicated the problem of meeting regulations

There had been no problem choosing an engine. Leonard Lord had already debarred tooling-up for a new unit and the Austin A35 and Morris Minor A-Series 'lump' was the only suitable one on the production line. Experiments with a two-cylinder engine—which was the four-cylinder unit sawn in half—took only eleven days to set up and little more to abandon because of the unacceptable roughness. Because there would be some unavoidable inefficiency in gearing between the crankshaft and drive-shafts, high engine efficiency was essential. The design of universal joints at the driven road wheel was another major problem for it was essential that there should be a constant-velocity joint capable of accepting wide angles of change while the wheels were being steered. If the joint resisted the attempts to steer the wheels while they were being driven, it would cause an uncomfortable or even dangerous tug through the steering wheel. Painstaking research by Hardy Spicer, now a GKN company, showed that precisely what was required had been invented as far back as 1926 by a Czech, Hans Rozeppa. The device had been made in America and the patent rights were picked up in Britain by Unipower (no relation of the kit-car company), of Shipley, Yorkshire, which needed them to produce joints for submarine conning-tower control gear. Hardy Spicer bought Unipower outright in order to give Issigonis what he wanted and started large-scale production, which has subsequently led to the manufacture of this type of universal joint for most of the world's front-wheel-drive cars today.

The first 948 cc car built had the fan and radiator on the driver's (rhd) side of the car and in prototype form was ridiculously fast in spite of its

31

Miss Great Britain, Sue Cuff. Mini skirts were well out of fashion by the time the four millionth Mini came along. Sue obliged the photographers by cutting one of her own skirts down

quickly cobbled construction. It had been clocked at more than 90 mph, which, when compared with the small Fiat of the day (58 mph maximum), was quite a significant achievement. However, it was decided to turn the engine around on its axis to give the inlet valves and carburetter (prone to icing-up) the shelter of the back of the engine bay. This meant additional gearing to prevent the car from suddenly obtaining a specification with four reverse gears and one forward. The change created a four per cent fall in efficiency and with a 100 cc drop in capacity and a last-minute decision to increase the width of the car (and therefore wind resistance) by two inches, reduced the top speed by an unexpected 18 mph. Another alteration was made to improve weight distribution, balance and handling, which came after high-speed, downhill testing. It was found that under very hard braking the rear wheels were so unweighted that they locked easily. The change was to shift the battery from under the bonnet to the boot and a rear-brake limiter valve was introduced.

Chalgrove aerodrome, a badly neglected strip in the Chilterns, was responsible for the late introduction of sub-frames. The first two cars, nicknamed 'Orange Boxes' because of their colour, had a sheet-metal structure part-bolted and part-welded to the hull of the car. But it was

The Italian job. Coopers on the left line and Innocenti-bodied Minis on the right in the Italian plant when under British Leyland ownership

found during a 30,000-mile, 500-hour test over the rutted airfield perimeter road that metal fatigue at specific locating points was rapid. Using sub-frames also presented the opportunity of insulating the vibrating parts from the passenger compartment, a ploy used increasingly in later years. Nevertheless, because the development time was so rapid, one major fault was overlooked. While pre-production prototypes were being tested in the summer of 1959, there was little or no rain. The fact that a stiffener was lapped the wrong way over a join in the floorpan was never noticed, but thousands of proud new owners noticed it in the first winter, and the distinctive aroma of rotting carpets became part of Mini history. The same wet winter also caused innumerable ignition failures because turning the engine round for the carburetter to gain protection exposed the distributor.

Issigonis himself spent sleepless nights investigating the problem of the slipping clutch caused by oil from the sump spraying across the face of the plate. New materials had to be found for bearing surfaces that could manage without lubricant so that the oil could be better confined to the sump. But with these nagging problems, and other more minor ones, the Mini went into production. All that was now necessary was to sell it.

A new assembly line had been laid in Car Assembly Building 1 at Longbridge, and for a long time it lay silent. Everybody on the three adjacent lines making Westminsters, A40s and A35 vans knew that a small car was coming. Not all were privileged to know what it was.

Albert Green was the CAB 1 foreman in charge of 1500 men. On many occasions he had been invited across to the experimental department to cast his experienced eye over the new creations taking shape and to pronounce whether or not there would be any trouble in assembling them. Early in 1959, he went home to his wife at the end of a long day with a secret to share. 'I've been working on a job today that, given twelve months, will be everywhere you look. You'll not be able to move for it.' Enthusiasm for the Mini was contagious and Albert Green, for one, could not wait to get the car into his charge. Ironically, when his chance came, he was not prepared for it.

Dick Perry, a man who was to rise to the position of Leyland Cars manufacturing director (and resign to join Rolls-Royce Motors in 1978), was the plant superintendent. As a management trainee, he had worked his way up through the factory and had only recently been personal assistant to Green. He came to Green's office one morning with an instruction from Sir George Harriman to build three prototype Minis. The assembly line was empty and the only labour available was at full stretch on the other three lines. For a few days, Green hoped the problem would go away, but when it did not, there was only one practical solution. He recruited his chief inspector, Freddie Finch, and appointed him inspector for the whole Mini assembly line. Then with a selection of borrowed tools, Green set to work alone.

He laid all the components for three Minis along the 220 yards of assembly line then started at one end and steadily worked his way to the other. Finch monitored and approved the work at every stage. Miraculously, everything fitted together and after seven hours Green drove off the end of Number 4 line in the first 'mass-produced' Mini. It was body number 101, engine number 101, white in colour and eventually registered 621 AOK. Some time later a second new purpose-built assembly shop at Cowley came on stream. However, this was turned over to Austin Maxi production in 1969 and all Minis were thereafter built at Longbridge.

Almost as soon as production had started in earnest there was need for a new department in the nine-year-old assembly hall at Longbridge. The joke that every buyer of a Mini was given a free pair of Wellington boots had become unbearable. Every car that came off the line was taken to the new area, where the sills were drilled and injected with expanding foam to cure the water leaks at a cost of ten shillings (fifty pence) a car. Foam filling of the box sections was very successful, and it gave an eight per cent increase in torsional stiffness for every pound weight of material. In 1974, Longbridge engineers recovered some of those early cars just to see how the foam had coped with a life on the road and found the metal inside the sections was still bright.

Green remembers many a fiery meeting with Issigonis, who had found no problems with his seam-welded prototype Minis, and could not

This idea came from the *Daily Express*. Execution was the responsibility of Morris at Cowley's public relations man, Tony Dawson. He borrowed 1,000 Corgi models to work out the problem in small scale before the stunt was set up on waste ground near the Cowley factory. 804 . . . I think understand why spot-welded production cars should cause such a problem. For three months, all at Longbridge had to grin and bear it. Production went on while everyone who could be spared hunted for the cause of the unwanted water. A watersplash was built beside CAB 1 and Perry, who was a demon behind the wheel, would drive furiously through the water while Green sat with his head under the seats looking for the source of the water. It took three months for the design engineers to realize that the metal plates of the floor had been lapped the wrong way.

The major production problem that the little car caused was lining up the sub-frame with the body so that the screws that went 'downhill' through the turrets would always bite on to their threads. A satisfactory way of squaring up the car was eventually found, but not before many threads were stripped and sub-frames scrapped. Every time it happened, the cost was twenty-five shillings (£1.25) and in those days, the total cost of assembling the car was only nine pence (today's four pence) more.

In 1960, by which time Green had been promoted to superintendent, the whole of Line 4 was manned by only fifty-seven men. Occasionally, they managed to assemble thirty-three cars in an hour, but they found that end-of-line checks took longer and the whole operation was more efficient if they stuck to twenty-four. One day-shift usually managed 180 cars, while the ten-hour night-shift regularly turned out 220. Every operator had a maximum of two minutes twenty-four seconds to finish his job on the Mini, so with fifty-seven work stations, one car took a little over two hours to be completed.

Green was often troubled by people from other parts of the Longbridge site coming to ask if the Mini they had ordered was built yet. He would feign personal service, point to a body at the beginning of the track and ask the man to return in two hours. In two hours' time, an inspector at the end of the line would be instructed to attach the relevant order to any completed car; and the harmless deception would convince the worker of the faultless efficiency of the assembly line.

The system of piece-work prevailed at the time the Mini was first being built and production was reliable. Twenty years later, the number of cars built depended enormously on the rate at which components failed to arrive because of outside disputes, and men were paid a flat rate. Twice as many operators were being used to build the same number of cars by 1978 partially as a result of industrial engineering studies. These studies came up with calculations which rated the physical effort required for each job and insisted that there should be at least 12·5 per cent of the shift spent relaxing.

In Green's day, man management was confined basically to finding jobs for a man that suited his temperament. 'You had to know who had the tricky fingers and could cope with the pipe-work. And the heavier work of fitting suspensions, for example, you would make sure went to the man who liked to get stuck in to a job. He is the same sort of man who prefers the heavy digging to the weeding'. Every man taken on was measured and it was guaranteed that the big man would not find himself having to go through the contortions of linking up the handbrake. A tall man would not have to work under the 'cake-stand'—the area in CAB 1 where the bodies were hoisted up off the floor for work on the underside. Green is slightly contemptuous of the social reformers who peddle the problem of 'assembly-line boredom'. He had more than twenty-five years at CAB 1, and the only time he recognized boredom was when there was insufficient work to do. When the line never stopped the men went home satisfied, he says.

Every time a new project came along—like the Canadian-specification Mini with its extra-powerful heater and additional emission control, it meant that work stations had to be revised. And when an operator claimed that he was unable to perform the task in the 2.4 minutes specified, Green would go down to the station and ask permission of the man to try for himself. 'Usually I was pretty sure from looking whether it could be done or not. If I was uncertain, I would say that I was too busy to discuss it that day and would give a decision in the morning.' He would wait until the factory was empty then go back to the line with his inspector and time himself on the job. If he proved his point he would prove it again in the morning. If he was beaten, he conceded the point. Although most of the part numbers for the Mini have changed at least once in thirty years and the specification had changed also, the tools and procedure have changed very little. Green did all he could to prevent any overtime being worked on the Mini because he knew how tightly the job was costed.

In 1968—midway through the Mini's career—the company could make only £35 on each car built and a mere three hours' overtime a week would kill all the profit. Rectification was not a large item, but it was this that was usually done on overtime. The most common fault was air in the brake system hydraulics. Engines were rarely worse than ninety-five per cent fault free. As time passed, the company compensated for wear in tools with increased efficiency, and quality improved by leaps and bounds.

Occasionally, a new operative would create a big problem. The classic was the one where a vital shim was left out of the clutch assembly and 150 cars escaped before the fatal flaw was discovered. All the cars had to be dismantled and repaired to overcome the problem of the rattling clutch. With 3016 screws, nuts and bolts in every car, it was amazing that the problem did not occur more often.

In the time Albert Green was the supervisor at CAB 1, he controlled production which earned the country about £7 million in exports. More than thirty per cent of that was earned by the Mini. In 1972, he was made a Member of the British Empire, and four years later, at the age of sixty-five, he retired.

3 Launch

The public launch was originally due on 2 September 1959, but at the last minute it proved possible to bring it forward a week to 26 August. By that day, cars had been delivered to showrooms all over the world. BMC in those days liked to describe itself as the largest manufacturer of small and medium-size cars in the world, and it was essential that there should be a concerted international launch. No one had given much thought to the problem of HOW it was going to be sold. Issigonis had fond ideas of a Mini outside every woodman's cottage, but, as the facts eventually showed for themselves, the appeal of the car was far more up-market than that. The type of person labelled in marketing jargon as working class, the little-educated, first-time car-buyer up to thirty-five years of age, only became a prospect for the first time in the mid-nineteen-seventies.

Austin and Morris franchises were still separate and the Mini was marketed in two guises. The name Austin Seven was selected to impress on the buying public the memory of the 1922 car, which was the most famous of all British cars built for the mass market. Just as the Mini was destined to kill off the bubble cars, the original Seven had put an end to the cyclecars that proliferated at that time. Morris Mini Minor was the full title of the car that emerged from duplicate assembly lines at Cowley, Oxford. In relative terms, this car was cheaper than the £100 open two-seater Morris built in 1931. Except for grill and wheel-trim differences there was nothing to choose between the two marque names, but BMC management went to the length of issuing the Press with two separate releases in order to retain the identities of two different makes.

'Penny-a-mile' was a theme that figured heavily in the first rash of advertising. The claim was based on calculations of petrol cost with 50 mpg possible at a steady 50 mph. The Austin Press release spoke of 'dart-like' stability on straight roads made possible by the rack-and-pinion steering and the stable suspension.

Huge advertisements appeared in the daily papers of 26 August which read:

The acid test. The Mini is exposed to the world's press for the first time at British Army's so-called secret vehicle testing centre 'somewhere in Surrey'

38

Right The hard stare of the studio lights picks up every blemish in a car but is invaluable for the photographer in this very early promotion shot

'You've never seen a small car like this before. Front-wheel drive. Fully independent suspension. Up to 50 mpg. Over 70 mph. And that's only the beginning. . . . Ten feet long, but roomier inside than many an £800 saloon. Yet the Austin Seven is less than £500 tax paid.'

'The Ride is a Glide', crowed the copy-writer. 'All wheels have independent rubber suspension so you get the silkiest possible ride. And because this is rubber suspension no passenger space is sacrificed. Front-wheel drive saves weight and takes you round corners like a sports car.'

The price was fixed at £496—a decision that mystified the competition. The cheapest conventional car built in Britain was the Ford Popular, which was £419 on the road. John Barber, the managing director of British Leyland who was axed by the 1975 Ryder Report, was working with Ford as a senior accountant at the time of the Mini launch. He recalls being amazed that the sensational new Mini was priced down to compete with the very old and very basic Ford Popular. BMC salesmen believed that with 3000 cars a week due to come out of Longbridge and Cowley plants, in which £10 million had been invested, the only possible way of selling the car was to drag the price down as low as possible. But the tactic just created an artificial problem. The working man buying a car for the first time—the typical buyer that Issigonis wrongly identified—is a difficult man to part from his money, and salesmen fought shy of getting involved in the tortured negotiations.

Meanwhile, up in the slightly wealthier middle classes, buyers were either picking up a better bargain than they need to have been given, or spurning the car because it was too cheap. Innovation never has been the ally of the salesman and the list of technical miracles on the Mini bred

The Issigonis obsession for space utilization led to the commission and design of wicker baskets to fit the shape under the rear seat. They almost went into production

caution rather than enthusiasm in the potential buyer. The good reviews in the Press did little to help the early sales, and the Mini was very slow to take off. The eventual success was unplanned good luck. It came when the Mini was adopted by the trendy men and women about London, who saw the Mini as the answer to their parking problems. The Mini's reputation was enhanced and rapidly it became the prestigious fashion accessory which spawned an era. One of the early fashionable owners was Lord Snowdon, who awarded himself a wind-up window but kept the standard production sliding window on Princess Margaret's side because it blew her hair about less.

The Press had been given a chance to drive the car on 18 and 19 August over the Army's vehicle test course at Chobham, Surrey. Motoring correspondents from all over the world were invited. Additionally, eighty leading luminaries were asked to take a Mini on loan for a whole year so that they could report at intervals on its attributes in service. The ploy also had the effect of getting the car noticed at all the most important gatherings in the calendar, which the journalists were bound to attend as part of their job.

In the early nineteen-sixties, the Mini's parking ability was of greater value than it is today. Meter-bays and multi-storey car parks are now laid out with each space big enough for the largest car, but when the car was new, the fact that a gap of only 11 feet 6 inches (eighteen inches longer

The launch of the Clubman. Leyland marketing manager Tony Ham and friends emphasize its virtues to the Press in the Longbridge hall

than the car) was needed for parking caused great excitement. Attempts to discredit the car, on the grounds that its interior accommodation was inadequate, failed. In fact the leg-room front and back was identical to the average space offered in the American cars of the day. Far more important, however, was the way the Mini stood up to scrutiny within the European small-car market.

The important competitors to the Mini were two British cars, one French, one German and one Italian. All the foreigners were rear-engined with rear-wheel drive; from West Germany came the Volkswagen Beetle, from France the Renault Dauphine and from Italy the Fiat 600D. The Volkswagen was the oldest of the trio, having been designed before the war and photographed as a running prototype in 1937. Just after the Mini was launched, the VW was to go up in capacity to 1192 cc to equal the Mini's 34 bhp, and the following year, the five millionth example was sold. The Dauphine was launched in 1956 with an 845 cc engine, in Britain was costing £796, and despite controversial handling characteristics went on to become the first French car to exceed two million sales. Italy's Fiat 600D was their best-seller even with its tiny engine. Potential economy was perhaps its strongest point.

Ford's Anglia 105E was not on sale until early in 1960, but BMC obviously knew it was coming and so considered it a rival even while the Mini was being developed. The car with the rear screen that sloped backwards introduced British drivers to engine speeds of 5500 rpm and Ford's first four-speed box. The Herald came a few months earlier than

'Good game, good game. Three minutes starting from now.' An early Mini comprised some thousands of individual parts, most of them being visible here

the Mini so becoming the first small British car with all-round independent suspension. That used the 948 cc Standard 10 engine and was available at £702. Sales were very low until Triumph got the might of Leyland behind it in the take-over of 1961.

A market survey run in 1960 by BMC compared the various abilities, and compiled the following statistics.

Turning circles:

Herald	26 ft
600D	28 ft
Dauphine	28 ft
Mini	**31 ft***
Anglia	31 ft
Beetle	33 ft

Top speed:

Anglia	76 mph
Mini	**72 mph**
Herald	70 mph
Beetle	68 mph
Dauphine	66 mph
600D	58 mph

Fuel economy average of *Motor* and *Autocar* results:

600D	45 mpg
Dauphine	40 mpg
Mini	**40 mpg**
Anglia	39 mpg
Herald	32.5 mpg
Beetle	31 mpg

Acceleration to 50 mph:

Anglia	16.5 secs
Mini	**17 secs**
Beetle	18 secs
Herald	19 secs
Dauphine	25 secs
600D	30 secs

In hillclimbing tests, the Herald and Mini came out on top. Both could tackle a 1 in 12·5 gradient in fourth gear. And on price, Morris concluded:

*Reduced to 28 ft in 1967.

'Compared with the cheapest rival which is the Anglia, the Mini owner gets free tax for two years, free petrol for one year and two free tyres.'

Power, at last, to the people. No longer was rapid and dramatic transport the prerogative of the rich. The young and the impecunious were now able to scoot round corners, hurtle away from the traffic lights and scythe a way through traffic. Obviously the Mini was capable of earning a name as a sports car and it did. Papers were full of quotes from professors and police officers who believed the Mini 'conducive to inconsiderate driving' and probably responsible for more than their share of accidents, and Mini owners did little to placate the public alarm. Inflammatory stickers appeared in back windows which read, 'You've just been Mini'd.'

Everybody wanted to be seen in a Mini that had something distinctive about it. Stage one tuning was to remove the hub-caps and fit one spot-lamp and a gear-lever extension. Wheel spacers were a favourite, which gave a wider track and plenty of opportunity for the police to write out chits for wheels protruding from the bodywork. The Mini-men responded with little eyebrow wheel-spats. Drivers who had the sense to wear seat belts found two immediate problems; one was that they could not reach the gear-lever, even with the extension fitted, and the other was that there was no way of reaching the central switches. Before BMC introduced its own remote gear-change, the conversion was offered by specialists like SQPR Engineering of Hampshire, who put one on the market in 1963 for £13 9s. 6d., which included a centre-console tray to conceal the linkages. The switch problem was overcome by the flexible plastic *extendaswitches*, which gave three inches extra length and bent rather than bayoneted.

Cosmic—the company in Walsall that made a name for itself with road and steering wheels—tried to sell a wheel spat like a cupboard door that covered the top half of the Mini wheel. That particular aspiration was burst by the wide-wheel trend. Nugent and Edwards of London thought that Mini drivers deserved a comfortable arm-rest rather than the sharp edge of the door bins, so devised a barber's chair-type rest that bolted to the bin and brought padded plastic to elbow-height; only 17s. 6d.

Another elaborate device with a limited life was the 'Thermal Control with Grille Shutter in Stainless Steel'. For £8 5s. you could have a replacement front grille which—from the comfort of the driver's seat—could be shut in winter for rapid warm-up, and opened in summer for twelve per cent better air intake than provided by the standard production grille. Introduction of the Riley Elf and Wolseley Hornet set one or two Mini owners pondering the advantages of a bigger boot. LBM Boot-Extensions met the demand with a £25 glass-fibre moulding which bolted straight on to double boot capacity. Seat extensions and steering brackets were the simplest accessories which gave the greatest benefits. Any driver who wanted to get the seat farther back for more leg-room bought the steering bracket as well, to drop the wheel a couple of inches to get a more reclined driving position.

Kenneth Baldwin of Surrey came up with a horn ring just like those on 'proper' cars, and performance enthusiasts all over the country debated

The unsinkable Mini converted to four-paddle-wheel drive for the River Severn Raft Race in 1977 by Longbridge engineers

Swimmy Mini or breast-stroke Moke. The amphibian was built for the Sammy Davis Jnr film *Salt and Pepper*, which was a satire on James Bond. The Moke had machine guns behind the headlamps and swam in the Thames

the advantage of Peco exhausts. The Fibrax accessory range included hub and nut covers to make the removal of hub caps more acceptable. In the mid-nineteen-sixties, everything had to be psychedelic and Minis were made to go faster with flower power. Another spin-off of the Elf/Hornet was the common aspiration for a smart wood-veneer mantle-piece, which was satisfied by many a coachbuilder.

Tilling Automotive turned out wind-up window kits before British Leyland made the move in Britain, and in 1968 was charging £24 for two. They were bought by those afraid of driving into the canal and having no emergency exit. Hard users of Mini Travellers and Countrymen found the double doors rattling unmercifully after a year or so of use. Intertech sold a single door conversion which had the catch on the pavement side and much improved the rearward visibility. Head-rests were just coming into vogue and the enterprising Kat-Nap rest suckered on to the side window for passengers who wanted to wake up with a crick in the neck.

Fiamm air-horns were a must for the aggressive driver, while Restall became the name for reclining seats. Toe-and-heeling specialists needed help because they kept missing the little pedal on the right and Speedwell—with the late Graham Hill a director—produced a non-slip pedal extension. Kick-plates lined the lower edge of the doors to stop winkle-pickers tearing the 'Connolly leather trim', and door stays held the doors open.

There were draught excluders, switch panels to fit the driver's door, oddment trays to fit as a lid to the door bin, glass-fibre panels, radiator muffs, radar detectors, hanging lanterns and nodding dogs. There were mud flaps and floor mats, headlamp flickers, 'Thoroughly Modded Mini' stickers, badge bars and nudge bars. They fitted roof-racks and hub caps, wheel-spats and boot racks. With pull-out indicators, press-on driving, push-in chokes, pull-in car parks, stick-out mudguards and stick-on ashtrays, there was barely space for the sun visors and brown trousers. Shops sold sills and grilles, back-rests, arm-rests, head-rests and replacement bodies. Minis needed axle-stands and hat-stands, a steering wheel and underseal, de-seamers and steam cleaners, air horns, horn rings, key rings and ring clips.

The little car caused the biggest boom in car accessories that there had ever been or ever will be again.

All dressed up with one-time potential dealer-fitted options

4 Mini-market

While most motorists have an adult-to-adult relationship with their cars, the feeling towards the Mini has always been that of adult to child. A child can be wayward but is always forgiven. A child can be bumptious and noisy but is never expected to be sophisticated. So it is with the Mini. It is cramped, uncomfortable, noisy, but it is also round, cuddly and vulnerable.

Sales analysis prepared for internal use by Leyland Cars in 1977

When Lindsay Campbell took control of marketing for the Mini in 1977, she set out to identify and rationalize the Mini's mystique. Her predecessors, in eighteen years, had developed no particular marketing policy. It was a question of capitalizing on events as they happened while trying to fend off the continual problems caused by inadequate supply and unreliable delivery. During the first year, the car had 'quivered on the brink of failure', in Mrs Campbell's own words. It had major faults such as the water leaks, clutch failures and gear-change problems. But as Ivor Greening, then manager of the sales training school, always told his moaning salesmen in those early days—under-development had been a necessary gamble. It enabled the car to get out early and before the competition. Remember it beat the Hillman Imp to the market by three years. The Imp was an interesting comparison because it was thought by some to be better engineered, but it did not have the same charisma. It was just a box on wheels and it never caught the imagination. Had it arrived first, it might have set the standard. However, it was a case of second being second best.

But the Mini, despite its problems, had plenty of image. As well as being distinctive by sight, it was distinctive by sound. A favourite sport among car buffs was to announce the approach of a Mini before it appeared. It quickly caught on as a status symbol in Chelsea and Kensington, and when the Queen took a brief drive with Alec Issigonis in Windsor Park, the rest of the country was ready to follow suit. Throughout the life of the Mini, the records showed that an increasing

Mini owners appear to be loyal to the model. Forty-five per cent of owners buy another

MINI 1977 BUYER TYPES

SECRETARY	HENRY	WORKER	HOUSEWIFE	COLONEL'S WIFE	FLAT HAT	BLIMP	AVON CALLING
10%	10%	10%	15%	20%	10%	20%	5%
ABC1	ABC1	C2D	ABC1	ABC1	C2D	ABC1	C2
–35	–35	–35	–35	35+	35+	35+	35+
F	M	M	F	F	M	M	F

MINI FEATURES

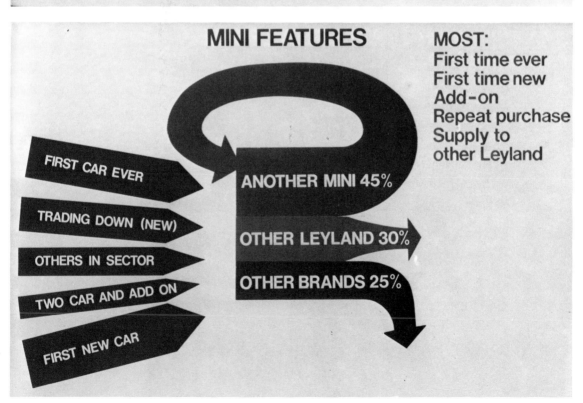

MOST:
First time ever
First time new
Add-on
Repeat purchase
Supply to
other Leyland

FIRST CAR EVER

TRADING DOWN (NEW)

OTHERS IN SECTOR

TWO CAR AND ADD ON

FIRST NEW CAR

ANOTHER MINI 45%

OTHER LEYLAND 30%

OTHER BRANDS 25%

49

number of owners were prepared to buy either another Mini or another
Leyland car. In 1976, forty-five per cent of Mini owners bought another
one, and thirty per cent bought a larger Leyland car. The age of car
ownership has come down quite dramatically in twenty years and the
percentage of female owners—in line with the growth of women's
emancipation—has increased.

BMC executives often wondered to themselves what proportion of
blame they should bear for the destruction of the British motorcycle
industry. While the popular theory was that the rash of cheap machines
from Japan was the culprit, BMC often thought that it had attracted so
many motorcycle and sidecar owners to Mini ownership that it had been a
conspirator in the assassination. The Mini certainly equalled one of the
main advantages of the motorcycle combination—the small amount of
road space that it consumed.

Mrs Campbell was aware that the Mini was becoming very much a
woman's car, for by 1978, fifty per cent of them were being sold to
women. So while it had to appeal to the fairer sex in terms of creature
comforts, it still had to retain some of the character that drew in the boy-
racer. The common emotion was 'fun' and all the Campbell-inspired
advertising emphasized this aspect of the car. 'Small' had long since
ceased to be a vital attraction and the word was substituted with
manoeuvrable. 'Joy-ride' was one catch-phrase, and 'Happiness is Mini
shaped' was another. Twiggy, Lulu, Spike Milligan; many a household
name helped to maintain the happiness image in TV advertising.
As a professional marketing expert with a background of selling
confectionery for Cadbury Schweppes, Mrs Campbell was conscious of
one major deficiency. The Mini bucked the determined trend that every
fashion object was taking towards greater elegance. Wherever she
looked—at cosmetic packs, cigars, clothes—the theme was long, slim and
elegant. Short, fat and dumpy meant cheap.

If there was no aesthetic advantage in the dimensions and few practical
advantages, then the economic advantages of small had to be analysed
carefully. In 1959, materials were a far more significant cost ingredient in
the manufacture of the Mini than they were twenty years later. In the
nineteen-seventies, the labour cost was so high that the variation in retail
price of a little car and a very little car was negligible. The final
consideration influencing any argument for a larger Mini is the name
itself. The trademark 'Mini' is one of the most valuable assets that BL
Cars possesses. If the car got bigger, was the word—and all the nostalgia
and goodwill invested in it—still usable? The Mini has been sold in the
sector of the market identified by the car people as covering any car with a
length of less than 160 inches. In 1971, thirty-two per cent of sales in
Britain were in that sector. By 1977 it was forty-one per cent. In 1977, sales
of the Mini 1000 were almost identical with those of the Clubman saloon
and estate combined. Both took forty per cent of the total Mini business,
while 850s and 1275GTs each took ten per cent. Five per cent were
automatics.

51

Opposite The subject of the picture is the Denovo wheels that became standard fitment on the 1275GT in August 1977. The little lady is sixteen—two years younger than the Mini when the photograph was taken

Opposite, below Minis as advertising hoardings. A scheme arrived in 1977 whereby an owner could rent space to an advertising agency and gain income and a respray

Multi-seat Mini, twenty feet long, appeared in the then BMC Piccadilly showroom window for Christmas 1964, with mirrored side windows and a caption which read 'Can you see yourself in one of these?' The plaything was created at Cowley with perfectly standard Mini halves front and rear. Seven people rang to place orders

It was not for its money-making potential that the Mini was saved from replacement at the end of 1977. When Michael Edwardes became chairman of the Leyland group he decided that the existing Mini would be kept alive and that the car designed to replace it would be 'stretched' to compete with new-generation mini-cars such as the Ford Fiesta.

It was not an Edwardes initiative. Alex Park and Derek Whittaker, the British Leyland chief executive and Leyland Cars managing director, had pointed the way to this decision. They were the Ryder men, the executives who took control of the company after the Ryder Report. When Ryder was largely discredited and Edwardes was brought in by the National Enterprise Board, Park and Whittaker left. But they had already agreed that ADO 88, the car unkindly called the 'Tardis' by those who had seen it because of its ugly looks and spacious cabin, should not be produced and that the Mini should continue. The decision was taken with the benefit of a new Management Information System, which for the first time showed the profit or loss on every car that left the gates of a BL factory. And it showed that the Mini was a loss-maker.

Throughout the period of BMC management and early British Leyland control, it was always alleged that this was the case, but there were always powerful vested interests arguing the other way. So the rumour persisted but was never proved to anyone's lasting satisfaction. Early in 1977, accounting methods at Leyland Cars (as it was then called) were changed by finance chiefs at Coventry headquarters. Colin Daniels, the finance director, was able to look at the performance of every derivative of every model in every market worldwide and see whether or not it was making a profit. And he was able to argue, without fear of contradiction, that the Mini was losing money. For the Mini alone, the

54   *The Italian Job* featured one of the most famous celluloid car chases of all time. The Michael Caine film had L'Equipe Remy Julienne stunt driving over rooftops, through sewers and down steps in Turin. Apart from the race track and rally trail the film probably showed the most exciting piece of Mini driving possible. Three Cooper S Minis were used, painted red, white and blue. Promotional spin-off was enormous

permutations of models and markets gave something like 5000 statistics. Many of them were 'fluid' in that currency fluctuations on the international money market turned losses into profits and vice versa.

Celebrated Leyland-watcher and journalist Graham Turner claimed in his book *The Leyland Papers* that just after the BMC/Leyland merger the Mini was making about £15 per unit. However, Daniels believes that accounting methods at the time could not have given an accurate picture, for too often cars were invoiced at the recommended sales price rather than at the price for which they actually sold. And in the later years of British Leyland, cars destined for export were sold internally to Leyland International, and the production side lost track of market performance and the return on its products. Daniels showed that while the Mini was making a modest profit in Britain (the 850 was priced at £1990 in May 1978) it was losing on exports and the overall balance was a financial loss.

It was not a situation that the accountants welcomed, but neither was it a signal for despair. For the Mini had other major advantages that established its *raison d'être*. Firstly, it provided an introduction to the range for the first-time buyer. The theory is that every major franchise needs a base model to attract people to become budget customers, then you impress them with good service, and as their personal finances improve you tempt them into more expensive and profitable motor cars. Secondly, if the Mini was suddenly dropped there would not be nearly enough cars to maintain the network of dealers. They can only survive by trading cars, making a profit on them, servicing them and supplying them with spare parts. If the car goes, so too do many of the strong links in the dealership chain. If that happens, BL Cars stops being the friendly neighbourhood dealer with a garage just round the corner from you

Above Opening the door might have been rather fun. The double decker Mini-bus was created photographically to stimulate buyers into specifying more practical corruptions like hot-dog vans

Left Shortened by nearly three feet and fitted with a Ford rear axle, this Duckhams Mini-can arrived at many shows around the country. Other users of the Mini as a platform for product facsimiles included Outspan, who commissioned a fleet of oranges—complete with a pip in each

Opposite, above Apparently all this luggage will go inside, but probably not at the first try. Yet another promotion for the Mini

Opposite, below Another promotional game. Many competitions were staged to establish how many people could be squeezed into a Mini. Records show that twenty-four may be the most

wherever you live, and the whole operation becomes less attractive. Thirdly, and most importantly, the Mini made an irreplaceable contribution to overheads. 'Economies of scale' has been a catch-phrase in manufacturing industry; in other words, if you want to make something cheaply, make a lot of them. That way you can negotiate cheap supplies of raw materials and afford to buy sophisticated machines capable of high-speed, repeat operations. The Mini may not have made money, but it did use 2.4 million wheel-nuts a year, enabling the wheel-nuts used for the Allegro to be bought at a lower price, so that the Allegro could be sold at a profit.

The least profitable markets for the Mini were in Europe, particularly the Low Countries and Scandinavia. In those countries, there is no strong vested interest in buoying up the basic price of a motor car because there is only a small indigenous motor industry. In France, Italy and Germany, the profit margins were not quite so short because Renault, Fiat and Volkswagen respectively had good reason to make sure the price of small cars was high enough for the participants in the business to stay in business. The reason for keeping open those markets where no profits were made was obvious. The argument is the same as for protecting the home market. Give the dealers something to sell and they are still there when you want them to retail something on which good profits can be made. Additionally, in Leyland's case, the level of exporting has always been a valuable bargaining device. Exports win foreign currency and make a contribution to the balance of payments. Bringing home foreign currency has to be the largest single contribution made by any British company. How could the Government do anything other than pour in rescue money?

Mini-cars only ever make mini-profits—or so it is argued. And it is a fact that if a car is only ten feet long, people will only expect to have to pay for it ten-fourteenths of the price of a fourteen-foot car. But it costs just as much to put a seat in a Mini as it does to put one in a Princess. It needs four wheels fitted and sixteen nuts tightened, just like any other car. There is scarcely any saving at all on the labour content in its manufacture, and very little materials saving. Since the Mini, a lot of people have joined the mini-car business, with Ford being a notable example with the 1977 Fiesta, and by manufacturing on a larger scale with fewer people and more efficiency, many of them seemed to do reasonably well out of it. The more companies involved, the better it became, for multiplicity always seemed to help in lifting the price base. In the late nineteen-seventies, small cars were experiencing a new surge of popularity inspired by the Americans. It was not necessarily true that a small car saved fuel, but motorists believed that it did and fuel-saving became a very important feature of car purchase.

Under the Michael Edwardes regime, which began in 1978, Leyland was pledged to de-manning. An initial 15,500 jobs had to go. The first loss was 3000 at Speke in Liverpool, where the TR7 sports car was being produced with such restrictive labour practices that it comfortably beat the Mini's record as a money-loser. The other 12,500 had to come from the rest of the car operation and the Mini sector was ripe for a slimming

This is another similar game

Glasshouse Mini (platform) at a Brands Hatch Mini Festival

58

programme. Comparing it with European competition, it was over-manned by thirty-five per cent. Although Albert Green shows that manning doubled during his period of experience, the two figures do tally because the car became far more sophisticated. With things like heater systems and dual-circuit brakes to contend with, it takes more time to put the car together. De-manning was not to be an easy process. Unemployment in Britain had been high for a couple of years and the unions fought for every job. The popular ploy of natural wastage—non-replacement of people who left—did not work. If a work-station on the Mini line was manned by twelve people, unions said it had to stay manned with twelve people. Management refused, unions instituted a work-to-rule and cars were lost. Such was the tussle that, in mid-1978, only 1800 Minis a week were being built at Longbridge compared with the target of 3000. Some days, a whole shift would pass without a single car being built, but also without the outside world being aware of a strike.

Mini UK price compared with cost of living

Date (October)	Total Mini price (£)	Index (Oct '59 = 100)	October retail price index	Total Mini price in 1959	
1959	496·95	100·0	100·0	496·95	
1960	496·95	100·0	102·0	487·21	
1961	496·95	100·0	106·0	468·82	
1962	526·25	105·9	109·1	482·35	
1963	447·65	90·1	111·5	401·48	
1964	469·80	94·5	116·0	405·00	
1965	469·80	94·5	121·6	386·35	
1966	478·00	96·2	126·2	378·76	
1967	508·75	102·4	128·7	395·30	
1968	561·10	112·9	135·9	412·88	
1969	595·50	119·8	143·2	415·85	
1970	638·50	128·5	153·8	415·15	
1971	640·63	128·9	168·1	381·10	
1972	695·15	139·9	181·4	383·21	
1973	738·84	148·7	199·3	370·71	
1974	1003·26	201·9	233·4	429·85	
1975	1299·00	261·4	293·8	442·14	
1976	1587·00	319·3	334·0	475·08	
1977	1893·00	380·9	384·2	492·68	
1978	2091·00	420·8	415·2	503·65	
1979	2404·50	483·9	486·2	494·60	(Mini 850 City)
1980	2683·60	540·0	562·0	477·16	(Mini 1000 City)
1981	2899·00	583·4	624·5	464·24	
1982	2899·00	583·4	667·4	434·53	(Mini City E)
1983	3098·00	623·4	700·5	442·25	
1984	3338·00	672·9	735·4	453·90	
1985	3598·00	724·0	775·3	464·00	
1986	3650.00	734·0	798·5	457·10	
1987	3725·00	756·0	834·5	446·30	
1988	4290.00	863·0	883·4	485·60	

5 Cooper and Downton

July 1961   ADO 50: 997 Cooper introduced
March 1963   1071 Cooper S introduced
January 1964   997 Cooper replaced by 998 Cooper
March 1964   1275 and 970 Cooper S introduced
August 1964   1071 Cooper S discontinued
January 1965   970 Cooper S discontinued
September 1964   Hydrolastic introduced for all models
October 1967   ADO 20: Mark II bodies for all models
October 1968   Synchromesh on first gear for all models
October 1969   ADO 20: Clubman-bodied 1275GT introduced
November 1969   998 Mark II Cooper discontinued
March 1970   Mark II Cooper S replaced by Mark III
July 1971   Mark III Cooper S discontinued

John Cooper, the World Champion racing car constructer in 1959 and 1960, was a good friend of Issigonis. In addition to having had the odd encounter as adversaries when Cooper drove his famous 500 and Issigonis the Lightweight Special, they had a professional relationship. Cooper was a customer of Morris Engines at Coventry for the engines used in his Formula Junior racing cars, and as technical director, Issigonis frequently discussed requirements with him. Therefore, when the Mini was under construction, Cooper was well aware of it. He and his grand prix driver Roy Salvadori took one to the Italian Grand Prix in 1959 and were amused to find that they had beaten Reg Parnell on the journey from London—and he had been driving an Aston Martin DB4GT. While at the circuit, the famous chief designer for Ferrari, Lampredi, spotted the little car and insisted on being allowed to take it for a drive. He was gone for hours and Cooper was concerned that Lampredi might have rolled himself and the valuable prototype into a tight little ball. When he did finally return he was breathless and excited.

'If it were not for the fact that it is so ugly I would shoot myself,' he said.

For the previous year, Cooper had been trying to find a successful formula for a four-seater road car that could outshine the two-seater Lotus Elite of the day. All his experiments with a Renault Dauphine body had failed despite the use of Coventry Climax engines and ZF gearboxes. The car just did not handle. Back in England, Cooper waited with bated breath for the first opportunity to obtain the Mini production version and once acquired he proceeded to tune it. He was convinced he could create the small, four-seater GT car and tried to persuade Issigonis. But the designer was still wrapped up in the idea that the Mini was a people's car and it was only by going over his head to George Harriman that a trial production run of 1000 Cooper Minis was agreed.

It was calculated that 55 bhp was needed for a top speed of 85 mph. This was achieved while keeping the capacity under one litre by increasing the stroke from 68.3 mm to 81.3 mm and reducing the bore slightly from 62.9 mm to 62.4 mm. The dimensions retained the flexibility of power output with twin carburetters and the compression ratio raised to 9.0 : 1, from 8.3 : 1. Although the cylinder size was increased seventeen per cent it was only found necessary to increase inlet valve area by twelve per cent. A slightly wider exhaust bore helped get the waste gases away quicker, and the bottom end of the engine had to be stiffened slightly to cope with the extra power. For racy gear-changes a remote lever was essential, and in making the amendment the Cooper raised second and third gear ratios to make intermediate gear speeds at 6000 rpm 28, 47, and

John Cooper (*left*) and John Rhodes both looking rather serious. Cooper obviously loved the Mini and was not slow in recognizing its potential

John Cooper in a more frivolous mood, this time with Dan Blocker and Lorne Green (from *Bonanza*)

72 mph. Lockheed seven-inch disc brakes were tucked under the front wheel arches to replace the inadequate drums. During the year that followed, BMC basked in the reflected glory of scores of competition successes. It tasted victory, and liked what it tasted.

Issigonis was by now enthusiastic and he plotted with Cooper over the next stage in the performance game. Through the late Eddie Maher, the Riley race-engine king who was the engineer at Morris Engines in Coventry, Cooper had been supplied with A-series engines for his Formula Junior cars which were far from standard. Externally, the blocks looked normal, but the bore centres were juggled around, the bores enlarged, the stroke shortened and the cylinder head given stronger bolts. For the planned Cooper S, the stroke of the 848 cc engine was retained at 68.2 mm and the bore was taken perilously close to its limit at 70.6 mm. The capacity was 1071 cc, which fitted in with the sub-1100 cc competition requirement. The short stroke allowed safe revving up to 6200. The crank was of EN40 steel especially nitrided by Issigonis's old friends at Alvis, and con-rods were stronger. To fit the bores into the overall size, a new block had to be cast with the two outside cylinders moved farther out and the centre two moved a quarter of an inch closer. From this was developed the rigid, closed-in block, without the tappet side-cover used on all non-1300 cc A-series engines.

The S was designed to rev to 7200 rpm with maximum power of 70 bhp at 6200 rpm, and the torque curve was far better than that of the standard Cooper. Rockers were forged instead of pressed and the valves

63

SLOPE Nº2
18½° 1 IN 3

TEST SLOPES

July 1961 — the first 997
Cooper undergoing handbrake
tests

had Stellited stem faces and ran in cupro-nickel guides. Head diameters were 1.41 inches inlet and 1.22 inches for exhaust. The oilways of the engine were enlarged and a bigger pump fitted to move the lubricant around faster. The gearbox was strengthened with needle-roller bearings on the mainshaft. More 'go' meant more 'stop' was needed again, and the heatsink of the Lockheed discs was improved eighty per cent by increasing disc thickness by an eighth of an inch to 0.375 inches, and diameter by half an inch to 7.5 inches. A servo went in and, for the first time, the Mini got wider wheels — 4.5-inch rims instead of 3.5. Standard rubber was 145.10 from Dunlop. As with the original Cooper, the suspension was unchanged until October 1964, when Hydrolastic crept into the whole model range.

The first *Autocar* test of the £695 car (£126 more than the Cooper) resulted in a 90 mph top speed and acceleration time to 50 mph of 9.5 seconds. A year later the long- and short-stroke versions of the S were introduced — 1275 cc and 970 cc respectively. The multiplicity of engines created considerable problems for Morris engines and first the 1071 — considered by some to be the best of the options — then the 970 were dropped. The best year of production was 1966, when 18,000 Coopers, including the S, were built — seventy per cent of them for export.

The BMC agreement with Cooper lapsed in August 1971 and the name died on the date of expiry. It was Lord Stokes who put an end to the

Racing patrons, *from the left* — Ginger Devlin, Cooper's racing manager; BMC's competitions manager, Stuart Turner; John Cooper; and Ralph Broad of Broadspeed

deal. Cooper's 'consultancy agreement' was one of several that were bought-out by Stokes after he took control of the company. His official explanation to Cooper was that the Cooper name was depressing sales, for it immediately meant high insurance ratings. It was a plausible argument, but the first thing that happened was that the successor was named GT — and the insurance rating stayed exactly where it was. Had Cooper not been bought off — and at the time he was earning £2 for every car that carried his name — there would also have been the Cooper 1300 (1300GT) and Cooper 1800 (1800S). However, in Italy, the Cooper name remained in production for a further three years because Geoffrey Robinson, the managing director of Innocenti, refused to give up his Innocenti Coopers. The end came soon after Robinson had been transferred to Jaguar in Coventry.

Cooper had been personally responsible for the advent of the disc brakes. He knew Lockheed was keen to prove the value of the system and thought that if they could show it worked as a tiny assembly inside a ten-inch Mini wheel, everyone would be convinced that it would work anywhere. Jack Emmott, Lockheed's chairman, needed no persuasion and went straight in with Cooper's idea. Cooper and his engineer, Jack Knight, were also responsible for the limited-slip differential, which improved racing competitiveness no end. He also takes the credit for the 'rose petal' aluminium road wheels that first appeared on his single-seaters but were eventually made commercially and in very similar form by Minilite.

Cooper's own business started in Surbiton, where it was founded by his father, Charles, in 1935. In 1961 a much larger facility was opened in Byfleet, but when, in 1964, Charles Cooper died, John decided to take

advantage of the interest shown by Jonathan Sieff, heir to the Marks and Spencer fortunes. For £250,000 and a promised annual £100,000 running expenses, Cooper sold ownership of the racing side while retaining control as technical director. Changes in policy at Marks and Spencer and lack of success eventually led to the closedown of the operation and John Cooper opened John Cooper Garages at Ferring, near Worthing. The property was one that he had bought as an investment with his windfall, and the part of the country was one he had come to know during his convalescence from the accident with the Twini, described later. He was helped in the running of the business by his son Michael, son-in-law Michael Angelo and daughter Sally.

Six of the best outside the Cooper establishment

Like John Cooper, Daniel Richmond was vital to the overall success of the Mini. While everyone else in the competitions industry was treating it as rather a quaint little joke, he was quietly getting on with the job of making it go better. His conversions became recognized, and his reputation was always that of being able to extract the sweetest power from the engine. The first successful competition Mini the company built

66

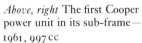

Above, right The first Cooper power unit in its sub-frame—1961, 997 cc

A close-up of the first Lockheed disc brake used on the early Coopers. Later cars used a much improved version although Lockheed did pioneer 'small' discs with these cars

in 1959, UHR 850, was kept as a showpiece and it was to become so much a part of the organization that it rated a mention when the company came to a dramatic end.

Daniel Richmond was a mild man with great skill as an engineer, even though he worked without a drawing office. The aggressive business brain was his wife Bunty, a relative of Somerset Maugham, who ran the operation with a rod of iron. Unfortunately, Daniel died prematurely at the age of forty-six. Bunty coped for a further five years, but told friends that she was 'phasing out'. When the daily help found a note from Bunty one morning it was to tell her that her employer was dead in the next room. In her methodical way, she had left precise instructions as to the way the crisis should be dealt with. The suicide note contained an instruction for Charles Griffin; the Downton Mini which competed at Spa had either to be found a place in a museum or destroyed by fire. Happily, Leyland Historic Vehicles had by that time found a home beside the Donington Park racing car museum and the car was placed there. It was displayed alongside the first Mini built on the production line by Albert Green, a Twini Moke, the Michelotti-bodied sports car, an electric version built by Crompton Leyland as an experiment, and Aaltonen's 1967 Monte Carlo car.

Richmond had built up the Wiltshire business, in the village of Downton, around exotic cars like Bugattis and Lagondas before the Mini had come along. He became one of the élite who plotted the Mini's competition success and attended regular meetings with George Harriman, Issigonis, Alex Moulton, Stuart Turner (the competitions manager), John Cooper and Charles Griffin. The meetings were frequently in a hotel or restaurant, where the discussions would develop into full-scale engineering explorations. Issigonis used to sketch frantically on anything that came to hand. Many was the time that he would walk out with a rolled-up table cloth under his arm which would find its way on to the wall in the Longbridge experimental department.

According to the people who worked with him, Richmond was an exceptionally thorough engineer. There was no magic in his engine work, just sheer persistent attention to detail. His engines were always spotlessly clean—a fact which, together with his oft-admitted liking for drink, gave rise to the rumour that he cleaned them with Gordon's Gin. Sadly, when the Mini ceased to be competitive, he lost interest in the business and devoted more time to his smallholding in Devon, to his passion of fishing and to drinking Krug champagne. That was not to say that his day was done. There were plenty of other demands for his skill, and he was still then collecting royalties from British Leyland for the MG 1100 and Austin/Morris 1800S cars.

Apart from its competition engines, Downton was building engine conversions for the special Minis BMC sold to the rich and famous— many at very advantageous prices in order to make sure they were seen in the right hands. Downton would have a standard Cooper delivered from the assembly line at Longbridge which he would prepare, before sending it on to Radford for coachbuilding. The delivery notes read like a section of *Who's Who*. The Aga Khan ordered a car; so did Prince Metternich,

Daniel Richmond exhibiting some of his handiwork shortly before his death. Downton-modified Minis were in a class of their own for many years

Steve McQueen, Dan Gurney and Lord Snowdon. Enzo Ferrari had one that he would take for a burst around the mountains near his home in Italy every time he felt frustrated or bored.

Ferrari and Issigonis were great friends and Issigonis would make an annual pilgrimage to see the great man. On these occasions, Issigonis would meet up with Mike Parkes, the talented racing driver whom Ferrari had adopted almost as a son after the death of his own beloved son, Dino. Before joining the Ferrari team, Parkes had helped play an important part in the development of the Hillman Imp—the well-engineered car that lost Rootes (bought by Chrysler) an estimated £9 million because of the success of the Mini. Issigonis had known Parkes, whose father was the boss at Alvis, when Parkes was an apprentice at Humber. Of course, Issigonis had been a keen driver himself in the days of the Lightweight Special (which John Cooper took great pride in beating in the 500 in a race on the Brighton sea-front). With Ferrari's

blessing, and with Parkes beside him, Issigonis regularly drove the latest Ferrari sports racing car along the road from Modena to Bologna and recalls with pleasure reaching 186 mph in the last of the front-engined Ferraris destined for Le Mans.

On one of the last visits to Italy, Issigonis agreed with Daniel Richmond that Ferrari should have an automatic Mini. Richmond and his wife Bunty drove the car out, but the gift was declined because the car was right-hand drive and unfamiliar to him. 'We completely forgot to make the conversion for him,' Issigonis recalls.

Many of the men who cut their engineering teeth with Downton moved on to found their own businesses. Jan Odor, a Hungarian refugee, started Janspeed, which specialized in camshafts. His countryman George Toth was the cylinder-head wizard who worked with another ex-Downton expert, Richard Longman, the most consistently successful Mini driver in the nineteen-seventies. Another racing driver who worked for Downton was Gordon Spice, who started life as salesman in the Downton London branch.

The Mini has always been a good friend to the autotest fraternity. Here Ian Mantle drives his Cooper to win the televised Ken Wharton Memorial Trophy Driving Test at Château Impney, Droitwich

70

6 Competition Mini

What excited the motor-sport enthusiast about the Mini was the quality for which it is legendary—stability. Few sports cars could corner at the same speed as the Mini and there was certainly no other low-cost family car in the same league. With a low centre of gravity and a wheel at each corner, the car had the basic make-up to allow tram-like road-holding. But that was only part of its success formula on bends. A word that is used by many and understood by few goes part-way to explaining the science of the Mini's good manners. The word is understeer.

Laurence Pomeroy, technical writer for *Motor* magazine, engineering consultant to BMC, close friend to Issigonis and author of *The Mini Story* in 1964, committed one of the best explanations of understeer to paper. He explained that on a corner, the whole car is subject to side-load arising from centrifugal force that passes through the centre of gravity. This is farther forward on a front-engined car than it is with a rear-engined one, and thus the front tyres are subject to higher load angles than the rear. The front tyres 'slip' more than the rear because of the additional load and therefore they will run on a very slightly wider radius. When taking a left-hand bend, the car will, therefore, tend to run out to the right so that more steering lock will be required at a high speed than at a low one to overcome understeer. If kept within bounds, understeer is quickly accepted by the average driver and turned to his advantage. When power is put through the front wheels, the ability for the tyres to resist slip under the side-load is further reduced. If the driver finds that the car is running too wide so that he is facing an emergency, his instinctive reaction will be to take his foot off the accelerator. Power is no longer going through the front wheels, so the slip angle decreases. Speed falls so slip angle reduces again.

Assuming the driver has maintained the same steering lock, the improved directional stability will make the car tuck its nose into the bend and the problem is resolved.

A front engine has two other inherent advantages. Firstly, it offers better car control for climbing icy hills. With the rear wheels spinning, a car will tend to skid sideways; the only means the driver has of coping with this is to steer into the skid and relax the acceleration. If he comes to a stop it is very difficult to restart. In a front-wheel-drive car, the drive wheels can be kept spinning while they are being steered, and momentum is not lost. With hillclimbing in dry weather, of course, the rear-wheel-drive car has an advantage in that the car's weight is shifted back so as to exert more downthrust on the drive wheels and get better grip.

Further, when a car moves through the air, it creates a 'bow-wave' just like a boat through water. This reaches out well ahead of the car and is where the second inherent advantage of a front engine takes effect. When deflection by side-wind gusts are caused, they occur by turbulence in that bow-wave. The loss of directional stability is less if there is substantial weight right up front where the trouble is. If the weight is all at the back, it is of little use in overcoming the turbulence.

The Mini fell into the hands of performance enthusiasts as soon as it was launched and many of them developed driving styles to suit it and get the best from it. John Rhodes was the fastest racing driver in a Mini for much of its racing career. His technique was as dramatic as it was successful. He would arrive at a corner with the car perfectly balanced and thrusting deeper into the bend than his competitors. When the car was drifting, he would lift off the throttle so as to achieve equal slip on all four wheels, then twitch the steering wheel into the bend so that the front wheels received a slight braking effect. That would cause the rear wheels

By pressing the trigger before running for his life, Leyland photographer Ernie Souch captured this classic. By the time Lincolnshire farmer Malcolm Leggatt finished rolling his own, the 1275GT landed where Ernie had been standing

Mini handling at its best. Irish grass-cutter Dessie McCartney at the limit of sideways motoring

to go light and the tail to hang out, thereby providing their own very effective braking while dragging the car round to point at the apex of the bend. This sideways style of cornering had even more relevance on the dirt tracks, which were the playground of rally drivers. If a car is thrown sideways on grit or gravel, the car's progress is slowed by the build-up of material against the wall of the tyre. Many rally drivers have kept themselves on the road, and in the running, by throwing the car sideways to scrub off speed. The technique is to floor the accelerator and the brake as hard as possible, so that the back brakes will lock but the front wheels will not. The driver can flick the steering wheel to steer into the bend to bring the tail of the car out, making the back wheels go sideways into the direction of travel while the front wheels continue to turn at full power away from the kerb. As the apex is reached, the line of the car should be almost correct for making an exit and the brakes are released.

Early exponents of the art used the handbrake to lock the back wheels only, but it is rare for a driver to be able to release the wheel of a bucking Mini even with one hand and even more rare that a handbrake can be a match for the speed of the car. The more proficient drivers, therefore, used their left foot on the brakes—a practice first perfected by the Finnish drivers to control the free-wheeling Saabs. BMC works driver Rauno Aaltonen drove on rallies with his left foot hovering over the brake pedal the whole time. He claimed that he would always approach a corner faster than appeared safe on the basis that all corners looked worse than they were. When the theory worked, he would stamp once on the brakes while keeping the power on and twitching the wheel

73

into the corner. The quick application would break the adhesion of the rear wheels by locking them briefly and destroying the balance of the car and the Mini would corner in the tail-out attitude. When the theory was wrong, and the corner was as bad as it looked, Aaltonen would recover from potential disaster with the continual left-footed application of the brake as described above. The trouble with the system was that having the left foot always in readiness to brake tempted unnecessary applications.

Aaltonen said that he was always ready to teach the art of left-foot braking to his greatest rivals because it took a long time to perfect, and while they were learning they would be overusing it and going a lot slower than normal—and slower than him!

In 1959, when racing cars were racing cars, the start of the saloon car race was the signal for the initiated racegoer to make for the beer tent. But the sight of Minis arriving at Silverstone's Woodcote corner all at once, and leaning on each other's door-handles was enough to empty the tent for the rest of the season and transform the attitude of spectators to saloons. For several seasons, before the professional became heavily involved, spectators were rewarded by people like John Whitmore, Christabel Carlisle, Doc Shepherd, John Aley and Bill Aston racing with not a hand-span between them.

'Up off the floor, navigator. You got me into this mess. . .'

John Handley knows that he was the first person to buy a Mini for competitions, for it was on the first day of sale that he persuaded his local agent, Darlaston Motor Services, to part with its only demonstrator. Handley had owned a Riley 1.5 up to that point, which had whetted his appetite for saloons, and when he first saw the pre-launch pictures of the Mini in the European Press he knew it was the car he wanted. The day he bought it, he took it to a meeting of the Hagley and Light District Car Club at the long-suffering Littleton Arms in Hagley. He said that he was going to go rallying in it, and his friends rolled around laughing. No one believed that anything so low on the ground could ever survive a rally. The current preoccupation in the rally world was jacking the suspension as far clear of the deck as it was possible to go.

Handley was not distracted. On the day of the Worcestershire Rally, he drove his new red acquisition, 4700 RE, to Worcester to collect navigator Tony Moy (who became half of the travel firm Page and Moy). On that first journey, he suddenly noticed that there was something moving in the passenger footwell. It was the rubber mat floating on the rising water. However, the Mini acquitted itself reasonably well in those early rallies, and was particularly impressive down hills, where its superior handling would put the fear of God into anyone. But more power was needed going uphill and Jim Whitehouse was recruited at Arden Engineering. He was very experienced at breathing new life into the engines of A35s and

Low-flying Mini joins the 1976 rallycross scene

Above Mud and Minis have always mixed to good effect. Once again their very controllability under such conditions is advantageous

Opposite, above It was perhaps in 1969 when this Equipe Arden 1000 cc car driven by Alec Poole won the British Saloon Car Championship from Abingdon and Cooper that the racing Mini was in its prime. Power and handling must have been at its optimum

Right Three-wheeling took over during the 1977 season of the 1275 class of the Leyland Challenge

76

Morris Minors and the Mini was basically the same proposition.

Once tuned, the breakages started. There was no engine damper and one of the engine supports, in those days, was the exhaust bracket. Every time the little car left the ground, the drive-jerk yanked the exhaust pipe off. The engine then rocked around so much that it broke up all the engine mountings. Then it was the saga of the wheel-centres breaking. Handley was one of a team of six Mini drivers entered in the Six-hour Relay Race at Silverstone. No one had ever raced a Mini for that length of time before and the drivers took the chance to become familiar with their new toys. The fast corners of the Silverstone circuit were all new to the little car and the cornering forces simply ripped the centres out of the wheels. It happened twice to one man during the course of the race, to Sir John Whitmore, soon to become British Saloon Car Champion, whose party-trick was eating beer glasses. The Minis were causing such a hazard to the race that they were banned. The first competition component produced for Minis at Abingdon was a stronger wheel; scrutineers would not allow a Mini into competition anywhere unless they had road-wheels stamped with the MG octagon. Within nine months of announcement, the Mini was becoming competitive. There was no one branch of the sport where it was outstanding, for in those days things were not nearly so specialized as they are today. People who were 'motor sports' did everything, and men like Ken Wharton were just as much autotest champions as they were grand prix drivers.

This rallycross car is not three-wheeling but merely landing. There never was a perfect answer to visibility, but this oversize fly-screen gave a clear enough view of the runway. Some masochistic drivers drove without screens at all

Good handling is well shown with this family of four 1000s in close contact

Doug Marsh in Kinver was the next tuner entrusted with the job of keeping 4700 RE competitive. The event was the Tulip Rally, which for Handley ended on the second test when the flywheel came adrift. Although it was a disaster, it was the beginning of something new for the young Wolverhampton driver, for he was talent-spotted by Peter Anton of the Victoria Carpet Company in Kidderminster, who was then the leading light in the MG Car Club and held great sway with the BMC Competitions Department at Abingdon. He told the shop that Handley should have a works-assisted drive and thereby started an association with the Mini which lasted ten years and with factory-backed competition that has lasted twenty.

His unfamiliarly taut and powerful little car was entered for the RAC Rally, where it was bugged again by mechanical trouble. But on the Tulip Rally in Holland that followed in May of 1960, car and driver came good and finished tenth overall. The most dramatic part of the following year's Monte Carlo escapade came on the Col de Turini section, where Handley clocked times as fast as those of Pat Moss, who was in a big Austin-Healey. Pat, the sister of Stirling, was big news in those days. She was more than just the best woman driver ever, she was also a match for any man. Pat also had the distinction of giving the Mini its first outright win in an international event when she and Ann Wisdom blossomed on the Tulip in May 1962. Another Pat in the works team was Pat Ozanne—who would only answer to her nickname of Tish. She was on the RAC

Rally in a works-prepared Mini only three months after the car was launched.

In those days, when the Mini was slow, unreliable and uncomfortable, no one really wanted to drive it and the established works-retained crews considered it a punishment to drive a Mini rather than the big Healey. That attitude began to change at the start of 1962, when the 997 cc Cooper appeared. Handley felt that his budget would not quite stretch to one of these comparatively exotic machines and he held his 850 together for nearly four years. The wait was worth it, for when the 1071 cc Cooper S arrived it was a vast improvement. Handley bought one and went international—dogging the works teams and sometimes embarrassing them. The Alpine Rally was the big one. Handley remembers the determination with which he and Tony Moy approached this major 1963 competition, where the timing was so tight that it was impossible to stop for as much as a cup of coffee. A petrol pipe broke and on the second night the inexperienced freelancers went out of time. The car that won the rally was none other than a 1071 cc Cooper crewed by Rauno Aaltonen and

Trail blazing in Europe in the 1960 Tulip Rally was a very young John Handley who managed a fourth in his class and was twelfth overall

Two racing drivers-to-be far from home. Warwick Banks gets a taste of rallying in 1961 in Corsica with John Handley navigating in a car bought from Cristabel Carlisle

Tony Ambrose—the first major victory for the big-engined car. Sixth that year in a 997 were Pauline Mayman and Val Domleo.

It was the last event that Moy did. It had been very expensive and he was disheartened by the run of bad luck. Handley had lost his co-driver and £150 on a short and not very sweet rally. He decided that fame and fortune must be awaiting him on the circuits.

When Handley arrived at the race circuits in 1963 he found that two men were on the verge of causing an upset among the established teams. They were Ralph Broad, who was a dedicated engineer with a tatty garage in Sparkbrook, Birmingham, and John Fitzpatrick from Birmingham, who was Broad's nominated driver. On one occasion that Fitzpatrick was unavailable to race, Broad put Handley in the car and watched with pleasure as he harried the established Whitmore, South African Tony Maggs and the 1962 British saloon car champion, John Love. That success led to the formation of the four-car Team Broadspeed. The idea was that four drivers—Fitzpatrick, Handley, Jeff May and Peter Tempest—should pool their cars. Ralph Broad was to do the preparation, and the drivers were to carry his name to victory. Right from the word go it was obvious the team cars handled better and went faster than the works-supported Minis. Broad worked like a demon—putting far more of his own time and money into the deal than he was supposed to do and over-engineering everything to be on the safe side.

Above The Don Moore-prepared car with oil cooler in the front and rear-mounted radiator

In 1964, the Cooper Car Company got the official works contract to run Minis in home events—having had unofficial support with varying bag weights of 'gold', since 1962. The team pinched Fitzpatrick, and Broad stepped into the empty seat to drive himself that year. The partner in the Cooper team for the escaped Fitzpatrick was a man already starring in other fields—Paddy Hopkirk. Broadspeed had a tough task because it had no factory money, but it did succeed in embarrassing Cooper several times. On occasions, Broad took the battle overseas and raced against the Tyrrell team of Minis, which was contracted by BMC to contest the European Championship. The Tyrrell drivers were Julian Vernaeve from Belgium, who cleaned up the championship in a 1275S, and the commercial pilot Warwick Banks. (Tyrrell was also running a Formula Three team that year with a precise Scot named Jackie Stewart as the retained driver.)

There were also Mini racers of considerable worth outside the three main teams. Downton ran its own car before concentrating on engine building for the Cooper team, and the European saloon car expert, Dutchman Rob Slotemaker, was frequently imported to make guest appearances on British circuits. A company called Alexander Engineering ran a car for Mick Claire, who had a dreadful accident on the way to Aintree for one race and was in a bad way for a long time.

Broadspeed was hard up financially by the end of 1964 and badly needed help from the factory. One regular gesture of help it did receive was supply of vital tuning parts from Morris Engines at Coventry. Eddie Maher, who was in charge of building Cooper and Tyrrell

An exciting Le Mans start at Francorchamps in 1965. Handley rushes for the car and . . . misses the door handle

engines, saw no reason to exclude Broadspeed from access to the special bits and pieces needed to remain competitive. Even so, the team was running on a shoe-string and was taking it easy in practice for fear of breaking something and not being able to race. Trouble with primary gears was a recurrent problem. Halfway through that season, Cooper had stolen a march by introducing the 1275 cc engine. However, overseas, Broad often managed to beat the Tyrrell team when he could afford to turn his team out, and the following year BMC decided that Broad should have the overseas contract.

It was the year of the three Johns. John Fitzpatrick returned to Broadspeed to race alongside Handley and John Terry stepped in whenever one was unavailable. Cooper retained Warwick Banks, who was runner-up in the British championship by the end of the season and pulled in that sideways-star, John Rhodes. At thirty-eight, he was a comparatively elderly protagonist. While being the most gentlemanly person he was the most aggressive driver, who always left the largest pall of tyre-smoke. There was a certain amount of aggravation about the terms of the overseas competition budget and the Broadspeed team became tempted to horn in on the Cooper act at home, much to the annoyance of BMC. Very often it won. Although there was a temptation for the Mini drivers to race against each other, the official target was the 'works' Anglias being piloted by Mike Young and Chris Craft. Broad was very cut-up when the advantage he had over Cooper was not translated into a contract for 1966, and he packed up his Mini bits and defected to Anglias. Fitzpatrick went with him. Warwick Banks transferred his interest to single-seaters and Handley joined Rhodes at Cooper.

Broad was always a very patriotic engineer and never considered Ford to carry the flag to the same extent as BMC. Ten years later he was able to

John Handley in the Abingdon car precedes the Britax Downton Cooper S of Steve Neal

make a nostalgic if rather short-lived return to British Leyland—having passed through a succession of racing Escorts and Capris. The move back was to prepare the successful Dolomite Sprints and subsequently the ill-fated Jaguar 5.3 XJ Coupé. The Rhodes–Handley partnership lasted two years with Rhodes getting it mostly his own way but Handley always right there ready to take over. For some reason, Handley's smooth, geometric and undramatic style of driving always gave him an advantage at Crystal Palace and whenever the track was wet. With Broadspeed out of Minis, the Mini competition came from Harry Ratcliffe—who made a name for himself by racing a curious American 3.5 litre V8 rear-engined, front-drive Mini—in the British Vita team car. Steve Neal, who became proprietor of the tuning equipment business 100+ at Tipton, often looked quick in a car from Arden Engineering, and Gordon Spice—who became better known as a Capri pilot—took a seat with Alexander.

The 1969 season was influenced heavily by the arrival of Leyland as the obviously stronger partner in the Leyland BMC takeover. Lord Stokes, whose forte was as a salesman, failed to see competitions as a sales asset. The competitions budget was slashed at Abingdon and three of the

KDK won the 1968 European Touring Car Championship for Handley and ten years later was in private ownership as a road car

four works rally driver teams had to go. Rhodes and Handley were retained for a limited racing programme, but Cooper decided to go on racing with the Cooper–Britax–Downton team despite the withdrawal of works sponsorship and entered Spice and Neal. Both teams made the mistake of looking for outright wins in a car that was no longer fully competitive. The Mini-man to see sense was Jim Whitehouse of Equipe Arden, who prepared and entered a 1000 cc car for Alec Poole and won the championship. Abingdon also spent money on rallycross that year — a comparatively cheap sport with good publicity returns when it was screened on television. The Minis were very competitive with their new fuel-injection systems.

Handley's last association with a works Mini was in 1970, when he was entered with Paul Easter as co-driver for the *Daily Mirror* World Cup Rally from London to Mexico. The car was sponsored by the BBC Grandstand team and the instruction was to give television its money's worth and to be leading at Lisbon or bust. It bust in Italy. The car was rushed home to Britain in time to be entered in the Scottish Rally. With Paddy Hopkirk behind the wheel, on his last job for the works team, it came second to the works Triumph 2.5PI driven by the long-serving British Leyland works driver Brian Culcheth. John Handley marked his departure from the disbanded team by buying the last works Mini to be built, SOH 878H.

John Rhodes was fired with enthusiasm for motor sport after seeing the great Gonzalez at work at Silverstone, but his racing started in 1960, when the impecunious engineer bartered with a wealthier friend, Alan Evans; Evans bought the car, Rhodes rebuilt it and they both raced it. Before joining the Cooper Car Company full-time, Rhodes had a very

Left John Handley and Paul Easter waiting for the off in the ill-fated 1970 World Cup Rally. The car was the last built at the Abingdon Competition Department

A wet track gives Handley the edge over Rhodes as he rushes to victory at Crystal Palace in 1968

close relationship with it through the Midland Racing Partnership. The consortium was building single-seater Cooper cars called Auspers— probably a dozen in all. The advantage was of sharing the costs of preparation and maintenance, and there was a purchase tax saving in buying the cars from Cooper in component form and putting them together. Rhodes was both chief engineer and number one driver, and

Above John Rhodes with
bar ed teeth holds off John
Fitzpatrick's Broadspeed Ford
Anglia

'Well Paddy, you get behind
the wheel like . . .' Hopkirk
watches avidly as his master on
the circuits, John Rhodes,
shows how

Above Was he pushed or did he jump? An unannounced John Rhodes speeds through on the outside as Steve Neal starts to spin, posing John Handley a major problem. Becketts, Silverstone, 1969

Crystal Palace again, this time in 1969. Spectators take cover as Handley hurtles through a whisker ahead of John Rhodes

could be seen driving in both a saloon car and a single-seater at most meetings. Even though he was sufficiently good with single-seaters to get a ride in the British Grand Prix in 1962, he never figured particularly well. His big moment was getting a works drive from Ken Tyrrell in his F3 team alongside Jackie Stewart at Zandvoort in Holland. He was quick enough to stay with Stewart for half a dozen laps, but the Scot was so consistent that he eventually shook off the most dogged pursuer.

From 1964, Rhodes was paid by Cooper to drive for them. 'When you have been round a circuit in a racing car, the Mini felt so slow. You could not frighten yourself however fast you drove and I just went flat out all the time. I was always struggling in single-seaters. Anyone who can drive one of those things quickly can drive anything. Saloons are easy. A saloon car man is not necessarily going to be any good in the racing cars.'

Rhodes always made a good start from the grid and on the first bend would lay out the biggest pall of tyre-smoke imaginable. The wily boys like Fitzpatrick would ignore it, but many competitors driving blind into the smoke would suspect that Rhodes was, at last, having his long-overdue big accident somewhere in there, and back off. Rhodes thought the most difficult man to beat was Geoff Mabbs, who had a most casual approach to racing. He would often appear in front of Rhodes at the first bend and display a *Sunday Times* and umbrella rolling around on the back shelf.

Brian Muir's frightened Ford Falcon tries to escape into the Silverstone crowd as a slightly bruised Rhodes rushes through

Rhodes was an old man by racing standards when he was at his peak. In his most successful year of 1968, when he became European Touring Car Champion, he was 41. A rather vulnerable man, he was drawn to the gentlemen of the sport. It was a relief to him when the tough and highly successful Stuart Turner quit as BMC Competitions Manager to be replaced by Peter Browning. Turner's style was to make all around him angry, feel wronged, determined and competitive. With a razor-sharp wit and massive grasp of what motor sport was all about, Turner was rarely on the losing side of any clash of will. Browning's approach was much softer. He was a quieter man, less extrovert, with far less experience in the business. He made his mark with Rhodes. The lack of ruthlessness clearly is no disadvantage in racing if the natural talent is there, but it did have its disadvantages when it came to business. While still racing, Rhodes made the mistake of opening a garage business in Wolverhampton New Road, near Birmingham, which he attempted to run by remote control. It failed, and although Rhodes earned £24,000 in three years from his annual £4000 Cooper retainer and various sponsorships, he retired from racing with little financial gain.

Sticky tyres is the epitaph Rhodes would engrave on the Mini's tomb after its death as a competitive racing saloon. Sticky tyres gave all Europe's super-saloons the same cornering abilities. Rotational speeds on Minis meant that sticky tyres simply overheated.

In 1969, the remarkable Richard Longman won the first race to be screened in colour on British television, and was then to stay loyal to the Mini for longer than any other driver and certainly with the greatest

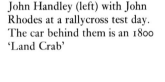

John Handley (left) with John Rhodes at a rallycross test day. The car behind them is an 1800 'Land Crab'

Opposite Rhodes kicks up his heels at a rallycross meeting

Fish-eyed and furious. The price one contestant had to pay for his entry in the first-ever Mini Se7en Club race date at Snetterton in 1966. Perhaps he was thinking of how John Rhodes might have handled it!

Rhodes venetian blind rallycross Mini. The method appears to work poorly

degree of success. It was a saloon car race and the Mini was being hotly pursued by a thundering Ford Falcon. Throughout the race, the commentator for the historic occasion kept referring to the fact that the Falcon seemed to be catching up. It never did, and the Longman crossed the line for a colourful victory in his ever-willing Downton 1300 Cooper S. That Thruxton win was one of the twenty-seven races in which he was victorious—more than any other racing driver for the season. Nine years later, in 1977, he was still writing 'firsts' in Mini history. His outright win in the RAC Group 1 saloon car race at Donington in August was the first win for a Mini in the category. And it was the first time in the Mini's eighteen-year race history that it had contested Group 1. Just to prove it was no fluke, Longman—who was then thirty-one—pulled-off another outright victory at Brands Hatch and in 1978 won the Championship. It was also something of a victory for the Leyland Special Tuning backroom boys and the unsung BL Cars competitions director, John Davenport.

Together, they had been beavering away at the unglamorous task of homologation—proving to the competition authorities that certain Mini options and accessories had been built in sufficient quantities to be considered standard production items. They therefore became eligible for racing in Group 1. One classic example was the wheel-spats, which are a standard part of the car as built for South Africa. Their use, in turn, allows wider five-inch wheels and tyres, which do not protrude beyond the bodywork. Surprising as it may sound, the carcasses of the tyres being used that year for racing were the same as Dunlop had

93

provided for John Rhodes. New treads kept coming. Technology stood still.

When Longman joined forces with Patrick Motors, the Birmingham Leyland dealer, to bring the Mini into Group 1 racing, Bernard Unett had won in a works-prepared Hillman Avenger two years running and was considered unbeatable. It had long since ceased to be a branch of the sport for clubmen; the season with the Mini cost about £20,000. An initial £6000 was to prepare the car; £2000 for spare engines; £2000 for tyres and wheels; £3000 for maintenance and slightly more for travelling expenses and subsistence for the team throughout the season. All that on the basic cost of a car. Certainly, permissible technology had reached fairly extreme proportions. In the quest for improved handling, Longman had explored the options of Formula One Koni shock absorbers—at £150 each. Handling was not a problem most of the time, for while the car was on the smooth track all was fine. It was when it had to put a wheel over the edge that the lack of versatility in the six-inch-long suspension arms showed up.

What did Longman himself contribute to the Mini revival? Well, just about everything and very nearly his life. He was racing at Thruxton when a differential seized and he broke a bone at the back of his knee. It should have been a routine injury, but he suffered a blood clot that stopped his heart twice. For weeks he could not speak, and he spent five months in hospital, during which time his weight dropped to less than six stone. But when it was all over, he went back to racing and to winning. In his usual modest manner, he puts none of it down to talent. 'Racing is like piano-playing. If you do enough practice you will be good at it. You get to know your car and all the bends of all the circuits.'

Despite his own disavowal of talent, he has shown it in plenty. In the 1971–72 racing season he drove a Lotus in Formula Three, sponsored by Security Express, where he was regularly a match for men like Jody Scheckter, James Hunt and Roger Williamson. But he had a big accident when he ran into David Purley's stationary car while trying to drive on slicks in the wet. The crash cost a lot of money. 'I had to choose between racing and my business and I chose the business.' The business in the seaside town of Christchurch became quite a Mecca for Mini owners. A tuning book on Minis published in America had said that Longman 'did Ford engine conversions for Minis' rather than 'he had once done a conversion'. As a result, he was receiving two letters a day from all over the world asking for more information on that subject alone.

Longman has engines in cars running in Germany, where a customer won a hillclimb championship, in Sweden, and in America, where the car in question won the Sports Car Club of America national championship. He has built the largest-capacity unlinered Mini engine ever at 1660 cc— beating the previous best of 1640 cc achieved by the rallycross exponent Tom Airey. It was done with a Gordon Allen crank—the longest-stroke crank that the specialist had ever built, and that engine went to Australia for drag racing; when fuelled by methanol it gave 125 bhp at the wheels.

On a slate-strewn hillside in the middle of Wales knots of anoraked

Opposite Function is everything with a rallycross car

Richard Longman leads a variety of group one saloons in the 1977 Grand Prix meeting at Silverstone. He finished second in his class behind Bernard Unett's Chrysler Avenger

Above Longman (*left*) and friends. Alex Patrick is managing director of the company that bears his name, and shares the bills with Longman. With him is George Toth, the partner in Longman's business, and (*on the far right*) Peter Wood, the Patrick Motors sales director

Opposite, above Richard Longman holds off a Ford Capri during a 1977 meeting at Thruxton

Opposite It was Longman who restored the Mini to the status of champion when he gathered up a couple of outright wins in 1977

spectators fidget round the unseen boundaries of their chosen vantage point. It's a scene of aimless expectancy with no diversions but the arrival of more pedestrians. But there is a keen eye searching the line of trees along the ridge and many an ear monitoring the echoes of the valley. The first sound is a distant whine. The man in the Castrol arm-band snaps round to his colleagues. Moments pass as they strain to hear the same warning, then a sudden urgency touches everyone. Latecomers, trudging warily up the narrow tracks, scurry up the bank, peering anxiously over a shoulder. Was it a false alarm? The trees and valleys play havoc with the varying pitch of a car engine.

It comes again—a new sound but related. A determined scraping and crashing like a plough-share tearing through rock. Up at the head of the valley there is a flash of aggressive Abingdon red and arm-bands gesticulate wildly. Round the turn and into sight comes the works Mini careering down the hill, bobbing tersely on its rubber springs, crashing frantically over the rutted ground. The metal sump-guard keeps it riding sleigh-like from the crest of one jagged boulder to the next. The front wheels scrabble desperately for purchase as the hands behind the screen writhe this way and that, slewing the car through the twists of the track. Now it's the unholy clatter of the straining engine mixing with the whine of straight-cut gears. The Mini winds down for the bend that the anoraks have selected to watch, grunting with each down-change and crashing more often on its sump-guard as the car's weight shifts over the front wheels. Then it flicks out to the left to shift the back wheels out of line and dives into the right-hand bend with the M and S Dunlops rummaging among the flints for a grip. As it disappears over the rise, the predominant

97

Left, top The Mini started its
rally career as the ladies'
weapon, and the most famous
lady in 1959 was Tish Ozanne
(*right*) pictured on the RAC
with co-driver Nicky Gilmour

Left, middle Paddy Hopkirk
and Ron Crellin heading for
retirement on the 1966 RAC
Rally. A Mini only once won
the British classic and that was
driven the previous year by
Rauno Aaltonen

Everybody loves a winner. The
1967 Monte winning car with
friends

Tony Fall on his way to tenth place on the 1967 Monte pictured here in a classic landscape

sound is the unexpectedly deep rumble of the exhaust bouncing around the trees and smoothing over the discordant crashing of steel against rock. There is a muffled cheer from the anoraks as they busy themselves with programmes to check the competition number of the car against the name of the driver they suspect was driving.

It was a bulky man with a broad face, grinning out of the helmet. The attitude was round-shouldered, almost hunched over the wheel—either the fastest-ever driver of Minis, Timo Makinen, or the lyrical Irishman Paddy Hopkirk. No external sign ever gave away the identity of the crew. Competition manager extraordinaire, Stuart Turner, never believed in teaming a car with one man. In the ten years between 1959 and 1969 the Abingdon workshop, alongside the MG assembly factory near Oxford, built sixty-six cars and a further three were put together around the time of the World Cup Rally in 1970. None of them were stamped with an individual personality. Most of them were capable of being pressed into service as racing cars, in addition to their rallying duties, and many were. Makinen's 1967 Monte Carlo Rally car, for example, became the favourite tool of John Rhodes for the 1969 racing season. Hopkirk's 1966 Monte car was driven the same year by the young Tony Fall on the Rally of the Flowers and Makinen then took it on the Tulip.

There was little sentiment about the cars. Once they had done their job they were sold, and even the Hopkirk Monte car, which was one of the team of four in the famous and controversial disqualification, was passed to apprentices at Pressed Steel Fisher. Few cars did more than half a dozen events. The little body was so rigid that by the end of one full-length marathon it was usually shot with so many cracks and splits it was beyond repair. Mechanically, the Mini was a dynamo. It always started and rarely stopped, but because of the small wheels and minimal ground clearance, impact damage was frequent. At every service halt, mechanics expected to have to replace disintegrated tyres, stripped drive-shafts or bent suspension units. As the jacks went underneath the car so too did the mechanic with the welding torch looking for the tell-tale hair-line cracks.

The Mini was very much a standard competition package because there was so little potential for variations or permutations. On a car like the Ford Escort there is lots of versatility for specifying engine, gearbox, transmission, differential and suspension. The Mini power-pack was a combined engine/gearbox/transmission set—take it or leave it—and there was so little room under the wheel arches once the disc brakes and chunky tyres were stowed away, that prospects for changing suspension were pretty dismal. The point came where it was futile trying to find more power. Rally cars of the nineteen-seventies doubled the maximum power-output achieved by the Mini in the nineteen-sixties. What it lacked in power, the Mini made up in cunning and tenacity. Most important of all, the people who drove for the works really believed the cars were capable of achieving the impossible—so they often did.

Whenever a Mini failed during the golden years of 1965–66–67 there was always another to take its place and, by sheer persistency, the results fell thick and fast. In that time, there were twenty-two overall victories in prestigious events throughout Europe—all of them the work of four men, Aaltonen, Makinen, Hopkirk and Fall, in that order of priority. Although Makinen was probably the fastest driver, he was very hard on his cars and the punishment took its toll. Aaltonen took the greatest number of wins during the three-year spell—eight—but young Tony Fall was the man with the win-or-bust killer streak. If he arrived at the top of the leader board at all he generally grabbed victory. Competitive spirit among the four men was a very important ingredient of the team success and Stuart Turner—journalist turned competitions manager who was to become Ford's director of public relations—manipulated and encouraged the rivalry.

Aaltonen was a man good at anything he turned his hand to. He was a Finnish speedway star as a youth, a speedboat champion and a grand prix motorcyclist. He was a clever photographer and had a very technical

It looks strangely naked without its front lamps but that partially explains the open-mouthed dilemma. Makinen was troubled with overheating at this stage of the 1967 Thousand Lakes. So he took the lights off and partially opened the bonnet to improve cooling. A big jump burst the bonnet open and the Finn had to finish the stage with unusually poor visibility. He dropped only nineteen seconds on the fastest driver and won the rally to pull off his hat-trick of wins on the event

Tony Fall blossomed on the 1967 Rally of the Flowers and finished fourth with Mike Wood beside him

mind which made him an interesting medium through which Issigonis learned some of the engineering lessons of rallying. Britain's non-specialist Press frequently turned Timo Makinen into an Irishman or a Scot by phonetic presentations of Tim O'Mackinnen or Tim McKinnen. He was a gruff bear of a man, round-shouldered and solid. He came to England knowing very little English and maintained a very clipped manner of speech. Like most drivers, he enjoyed unwinding with as much abandon as he drove and was frequently at the centre of the wilder parties in rally hotels. Paddy Hopkirk was to rallying what Stirling Moss was to British racing. His meticulous self-promotion was a discipline designed to make him a household name, and it worked, for he has built a car accessory empire by branding goods with his own name. He was well liked by the popular Press because he could always toss off a gem of a quote in any situation. Tony Fall joined the team last and never really became one of the terrible trio. But his three years with BMC, ending when the team was disbanded, was the highspot of his rallying career. Thereafter he was blighted by unreliability and misfortune, but turned to rally management and found a very senior berth with Opel in Germany.

Close communication was vital in the BMC team and one of the refinements of communications that the Mini-men developed was pace notes. In the European rallies where practising was permitted, crews would go out days in advance to plot all the corners of the route and ice crews would go out again just before a section was due to be run to update the information with ice notes. Armed with this vital information—fed to him by his co-driver through an intercom, which was the only way of beating the engine noise—a driver could go flat out into a bend with the confidence of knowing what conditions to expect on the other side.

On the 1966 Alpine, Paddy Hopkirk was driving flat out through a pea-souper fog with Ron Crellin beside him calmly telling him the tale. Belting down the Col d'Iseran they actually overtook the rally leader. Their event that year, sadly, ended in retirement. Rauno Aaltonen gave the pace notes system much of the credit for his outright win on the Monte Carlo rally the following year. The downhill Col de Turini was sheet ice, conditions were thick fog, the penalty of a mistake was a 3000-foot drop, but with Henry Liddon reading the notes, Aaltonen was able to drive the whole section blind.

By the time the team had standardized on the shorthand they used to denote '90 left over brow' and so on, they were able to send one team to do the research and let all the others use the same notes. Paddy Hopkirk and Henry Liddon recced the Alpine together in 1965. One particular bend on the Col de Granier gave them endless problems. They could not agree on the grading of an unusually severe corner that looked like a 'medium left'. Eventually they decided to amend 'medium left' with the exclamation 'and how'. The instructions were photostated and handed round to the other teams. Come the day of reckoning, Tony Ambrose reached the controversial section of the notes while Rauno Aaltonen careered into the bend at full chat. After a split-second delay that lasted a life-time, Ambrose stammered the translation of Liddon's handwriting;

Irish ingenuity rules. Paddy Hopkirk masterminds a spot of underbody servicing on his way to winning the 1967 Acropolis Rally. Co-driver was Ron Crellin

The winning car does a whirl for the cameras

Opposite One of the most famous shots of them all. The fiery, fuel-injected car was built for the cancelled 1967 RAC Rally and ran on the retained televised special stage. Makinen drives, Tony Fall wonders

'medium left and house'. The imperilled flight into the corner continued unabated with Aaltonen scanning the road for this all-important house. By the time the two men realized something had gone wrong, they were airborne and their chances of the Coupe des Alpes and the Touring Car Class prize were in serious jeopardy. By chance, the landing was soft and the road regainable. They won both awards.

On the occasions that the precision of communication was not quite so vital, the boisterous Timo Makinen could not resist using it for his amusement. When, in 1965, the young Swedish driver Jorma Lusenius came to Britain for a trial drive in the RAC Rally (and finished a creditable sixth) he was assigned Mike Wood as co-driver. The problem was that the two men had no common language so Stuart Turner decided they should have a two-day getting-to-know-you session in Wales. Mike Wood mapped out a few key phrases he thought they might need like 'left', 'right', 'fast' and 'slow', 'pint', 'half a pint', 'fill her up' and 'how old is your daughter?' Makinen was asked to list the Swedish translations, which he did with considerable enthusiasm but not in the same order as the original. The first thing the Lusenius/Wood crew learned was how to reverse out of uncomfortable situations.

Very often in motor sport, the conclusion of an event is not at the end of the last time stage but in the appeal courts of the governing body of the sport. Never was this more true than during the reign of the Mini. Rival manufacturers with far more powerful cars felt they had been cheated by the Mini and wanted to see the Mini's case tested and proved. Most cynical of all were the chauvinistic French. Twice running in 1964 and 1965 the little cars had been to the prestige event in Monte Carlo and carried all before them. The Frenchmen—and more particularly the Monégasque organizers—were determined that BMC should not complete the hat-trick in 1966. Obstacles were placed in the way of the English team well before its arrival in the Mediterranean principality. Usual practice was to run the event on a handicap system so that a car from any class—Groups 1, 2 or 3—had an equal chance of success. In

Opposite The one that faded away ... 1968 saw Makinen's three team-mates finish third, fourth and fifth behind two Porsches, but Makinen lost a crankshaft pulley and arrived in Monte Carlo with a white-hot engine

Right The final event for a works Mini. Hopkirk pulled off a strong second place on the 1970 Scottish Rally

1966, the system was changed in such a way that it was obvious only a Group 1 car had any chance of overall victory. Minis had always been in Groups 2 or 3—the classes for modified cars. The prerequisite for qualifying for Group 1 was that the car must be (virtually) in standard production form, and 'production' meant that the manufacturer must have made 5000 within the previous twelve months. The previous year, the figure had been 1000.

In those halcyon days—competition was everything. Stuart Turner had a word in the right ear and, as the build figures show, production was speeded up. By the qualifying date, BMC had built 5047 Cooper S models and were therefore eligible to compete with it as a standard production car. It was without many of its demon tweaks, but then that applied also to all the rivals. When the team arrived in Monte Carlo, the hostility was intense. Whenever the French Press inquired as to the aim of the team, the reporter was told that BMC was out for overall victory—not a class win. The reply was always a shrug and a wave of the arms. It was clear that no one with his ear to the ground expected the environment to favour the Minis. Timo Makinen thought otherwise and there is nothing more determined than a disgruntled Makinen. From the word go he was flying. In the early stages he was beating the hairiest of Group 3 sports cars and was arriving at stage finish lines so fast that twice he found officials unready.

At the end of the first day Makinen was leading, Aaltonen was right up with him and he and Hopkirk had caught two Lotus-Cortinas in a sandwich. One was Roger Clark—the best-ever British rally driver—and the other was Bengt Soderstrom, who was to win the RAC Rally later that year. In the final eleven hours through nearly 400 miles of tight mountain circuits, Hopkirk pulled the Ford pair back and, in the run down to the finish, made it a clean sweep of Minis first, second and third; a hat-trick of wins in the most dramatic style possible. The winning cars went straight to the routine scrutineering, where their legality was checked against the list of standard equipment BMC said was built in to every Cooper S sold over the counter.

For eight hours, the demoralized French officials pored over the cars.

Monotonously, they found first one irregularity then another, only to have to withdraw the allegations once the BMC team managers impressed them with the facts. Finally the results were posted. The proud Mini crews drew close to learn by how great a margin they had stolen victory. There, at the top of the honours sheet, was a Citroën. Stuart Turner was aghast. For an hour—while the French Press flashed off their tributes to the waiting nation—he had to bite his tongue. At last the explanation came in the form of an accusation. The lights of all three Minis failed to conform with the regulations of the sport. The worst had been confirmed. The organizers had played a hand of which they had given notice during the event. At the end of the first day, they had posted an announcement at rally headquarters suggesting that some cars—all the British entrants among them—might not comply with international highway regulations in respect of the dipping arrangements of the headlamps. After an impromptu check had been run on every car, a second notice had gone up describing the light pattern of each. It had carried a rider saying that the acceptability of each light pattern would be decided at final scrutineering.

The BMC team had wondered and worried and discounted the idea that a feature so irrelevant to the performance of a car could find a place in the final reckoning. But it had, and no amount of appeal to the organizers, to the Monaco Auto Club or to the world governing body of motor sport (in Paris) could reverse the decision. The accusation was plain. The English had cheated and had to be punished. Having been denied the rich spoils of victory they were even deprived of a finisher's plaque. One French organ, the sporting paper *L'Equipe*, remained open-minded about the extent to which BMC had campaigned non-standard cars. At the suggestion of BMC, it administered a run-off between Hopkirk's car and a standard Cooper S taken straight from the showroom in Monte Carlo. The drivers were to be Timo Makinen and Alain Bertaut, a motoring journalist on *l'Action Automobile* and *Moteur*, who was a seasoned racing driver. The course was a hillclimb chosen by *L'Equipe*. If Makinen could beat the works car in the shiny showroom demonstrator, surely that would be enough proof that there was nothing outstanding or dishonest about BMC's preparation for the rally?

In the event, both drivers put up quicker times over the course in the untouched road car. The point was proved, but the officials of the Monte Carlo Rally were unimpressed. What BMC gained out of it all was worldwide publicity in best 'we-was-robbed' style, and a thunderous welcome home at London Airport. There was only one complete answer to the tactics adopted in Monte Carlo. The following year, BMC sent a team of five cars with Tony Fall and Simo Lampinen running four and five. Rauno Aaltonen gave the performance of a lifetime and with a judicious piece of tyre selection, which gave him the edge on the rest of the team, carried off the victor's trophy. So BMC got its third official win at Monte, and in achieving it, each of the mischievous *Three Musketeers*, the same three men declared outlaws in 1966, took one victory. Just taste that revenge!

It would be undesirable to create the impression that the BMC rally

A sorry sight at Abingdon. In 1970 the famous competition workshop was turned over to commercial tuning work

men were totally above any unusual interpretation of the rules. The spirit of competition in motor sport does not demand 'Thou shalt not cheat'; only 'Thou shalt not be caught at it.' During the 1967 Italian Rally of the Flowers, Paddy Hopkirk did and he was not. The last competitive stage of the event finished nearly thirteen miles from the final control in the coastal town of San Remo and Hopkirk was leading the event. A mile from the end of that stage, Hopkirk's Mini broke a drive-shaft coupling and had to be pulled out by tractor. The stage time cost him his lead, but he was not out of the running until he failed to show up at the final control! A shove over the brow of the hill enabled him to meet up with his service crew in a big 4-litre Princess manned by the new competitions manager, Peter Browning, and mechanic Doug Watts. They had a spare coupling aboard but not the time to fit it. Hopkirk did not hesitate. He ordered navigator Ron Crellin back aboard the Mini and demanded a shove from the Princess, which then kept station astern until needed again. The two cars careered off in tandem with the little car running away from the massive front bumper on the steep descents and being collected up again every time the pace slowed. At the first sight of cheering crowds or lurking photographers the two cars would part magically, Hopkirk would play a tune on the gearbox and blip the throttle. Around the next corner

Above Leg-out-of-bed, would-be rallycross expert rolls expensively towards the bank

Opposite, above Gordon Rogers was a rallycross newcomer in 1976 but with his self-prepared Mini swamped many of the old hands and finished fourth in the Embassy series

Minis racing in supersaloon classes either did not look like Minis or retained some semblance of the original car in order to please sponsors, in which case they were rarely successful

the coming together would be enacted with a resounding crash. It worked like a dream until the time came to check into a passage control. Doug Watts gave the Mini a parting shove then overtook, drove anonymously through the passage control, and parked up round the first bend.

The two men waited with bated breath, fearing that at any moment rally officials would round the corner and point accusing fingers. But the first arrival was Hopkirk, revving the engine gamely, and drifting down the gentle incline with a feigned slipping clutch. The final obstacle was the town itself, built on flat ground, crowded with spectators and approached through a long, dark tunnel. With Ron Crellin in the co-driver's seat gesticulating wildly for more speed to beat the clock at the last control, Watts accelerated up to sixty mph then flung the Mini out into the daylight. Driving with no power through the wheels and perilous handling, Hopkirk somehow managed to thread a way through the streets, squeal round a signalling policeman on point duty, and drift into the control area. His time gave him second place in the rally and although the last couple of miles had been watched by hundreds of people, international Press, police, officials and television cameras nobody ever guessed or challenged. The truth was not confessed for four years, until 1971, by Peter Browning.

Above Leyland Challengers in formation

Above, right Richard Longman weighed into the Mini's 20th anniversary year by winning the British Saloon Car Championship. The win came on 29 September at Oulton Park in a twin carb car sponsored by Patrick Motors of Birmingham. Longman, who was 33, had won the BARC Saloon Car Championship in a Cooper S ten years earlier

Below, right Charles Berstein of Birmingham knew how to pick up a winner. In 1979 his lightweight special clinched the Brush Fusegear Special Saloon Car Championship

Left Upside-down Mini

7 The tyre and automatic story

Beside Issigonis's desk at Longbridge were stacked five Morris Minor wheels and tyres. He also had four hard-backed chairs which he would arrange to demonstrate how compactly four people could be packaged. In discussions with tyre and suspension engineers, the conversation would always return to the demands on space made by people and wheels. One day he waved angrily at the pile of wheels. 'Why the hell do you people need such huge wheels. You must squeeze them down to this size,' he admonished, holding his hands only a few inches apart.

Tom French, the brilliant Dunlop designer who was later to be responsible for the Denovo run-flat tyre, remembers the stunned silence as the suspension and tyre engineers regarded the area enclosed by Issigonis's outstretched hands. Then somebody—French cannot remember who—took a ruler and measured the indignant Issigonis. The target was set.

'We considered eight inches as a thinking exercise, but it was never really very serious because there was no room for the brakes. We looked at eleven inches as well, before deciding to make the rubber for ten-inch wheels.'

Dunlop's development of tyres and wheels was a cliff-hanger which lasted as long as the development of the car itself. There is no substitute for prolonged testing in tyre design. And had Dunlop turned round to Issigonis in those early days and said wheels smaller than the fourteen-inches of the Minor were not possible, then the Mini project would have been dead. BMC and Dunlop had a very close, very personal relationship in the nineteen-fifties. Both companies believed in the British ethos and were committed to doing something for British industry. It was therefore to Dunlop that Issigonis turned. Had the company failed him, it is unlikely that Issigonis would have persevered with the idea.

'He was not interested in the technicalities. He just wanted us to get on with the job. Issigonis only ever gave you a few moments to understand

The rear-engined, two-cylinder Goggomobil was used by Dunlop to test the wheels and tyres needed for the Mini. This car was built in Germany in 1955

him. He was not a man to suffer fools at all. Once accepted, you were trusted to provide what was required,' French remembers.

Dunlop was lucky in having as sales director the late Jimmy Dorr, an erudite, convincing man with a degree in technical sciences. He was able to talk to Issigonis and to introduce Tom French. French decided that the job could be done, and as the research progressed, the severe Ted Masheter, technical director and a board member with Dorr, became convinced also. No sudden decision to risk the massive investment was needed to supply a completely new type of wheel and tyre. There was simply a well-reasoned drift towards the inevitable.

Dunlop's managing director at that time was Sir Edward G. Beharrell, whose previous career and general attitude were such as to approve of innovation. The main concern about the little tyres was that they would disintegrate because of the high rotational speed and planned performance of the car. These fears were exacerbated by two brilliant research engineers, Willy Kramer and Ralph Kuttesmichel, in Dunlop's German sister company. Germany was building both autobahns and ludicrous, small-wheeled bubble cars, and tyre failures on Europe's first motorways were legion. The two Germans objected to the little wheels all the way along the line, forcing French to strengthen his case.

Issigonis made life even more difficult by insisting that tyre life was not bought at the expense of grip. Up to this point, cars generally did not corner well and when the trend changed, tread life took a dive. Cross-ply tyres were not an ideal partner for front-wheel drive, a problem Michelin, in France, had worried about on behalf of Citroën, its partial subsidiary. By playing with construction and compounds, French was able to raise tread wear to an acceptable level, but still had to pass for production a

113

The 1275GT was the first small car to have the Denovo run-flat tyre as optional equipment

tyre which was inferior in life expectancy to the Minor tyres. He knew that in some hands the front covers would only do 6000 miles, but encouraged himself with the knowledge that they could be interchanged with rear tyres, which the worse treatment could not drag below 15,000. The average life for the set of tyres was expected to be 22,000 miles, compared with 26,000 for the Minor. It was not to be until the early nineteen-sixties that the introduction of Mini-sized radials sent the figures soaring.

Security of the tyre on the rim was another worry, for the beading length was twelve inches shorter than on the Minor tyre. The decision had already been taken to follow the development going ahead for Jaguar—namely in tubeless tyres. This increased the danger if there was going to be any bead displacement; so a wider ledge was designed and the problem overcome.

The Mini set a high standard for steering response, but there was criticism that it 'darted' too much over white road markings. This was an inevitable consequence of building quick response into the steering, but after further development Dunlop alleviated the problem by building a safety shoulder into the tyre to dampen the effect.

During the testing of the tyres, Dunlop was unable to get hold of a prototype Mini until very shortly before the launch. So they used a much-modified German Goggomobil to pack in the road mileage. The firm had to fit it with a very extravagant driving seat because the test drivers threatened to strike over the disc-slipping discomfort of the ride.

In the spring of 1959, Tom French was able to take a prototype Mini to Sweden to check cold-weather and snow and ice performance, under the control of BMC development engineer Gill Jones. Shortly after the exercise, a scoop photograph of the Mini appeared in the European magazine *L'Auto Journal*. How a car fell victim to the spyman's lens remains a mystery, but French is adamant it was not the Swedish car that 'leaked'.

Ian Mills, who became senior product manager with Dunlop and then Meriden MP, remembers his days as chief racing tyres designer with some discomfort. The cause of that was not so much the Formula One arena, where drivers such as Graham Hill, John Surtees and Jim Clark were locked in deadly combat, but Mini racing. 'I had more sleepless nights worrying about the Minis than about anything else,' he recalls.

In 1965, when the power output of the racing Mini Cooper was nudging 100 bhp, the racing tyres could no longer take the pace. On some of the adverse camber bends at Brands Hatch, for example, the quick Minis were lifting an inside drive-wheel and the smoke which poured off the spinning tyre bore witness to rubber temperatures approaching 130 degrees centigrade—well above boiling point and much hotter than the temperatures experienced by Formula One tyres.

A bit of heat is a good thing, it makes the tyre surface sticky and improves adhesion. That is why racing drivers blip the throttle and drop the clutch to create wheelspin on the warm-up lap approach to the startline. But very high temperatures just mean that the tyres lose their stability and grip. In those days of Mini racing, the little car would hurtle off the line into an instant lead and for two or three laps make mincemeat of the opposition. Then, as the tyres deteriorated, the bigger cars would haul them in and go past.

Higher management at Dunlop was very conscious of the special relationship with BMC and of the need to do all it could to keep the Mini a winner. So word came down to Iain Mills, appointed to the hot seat in 1966, that no expense should be spared in putting good rubber under the Mini, in spite of the many phases of experiment before his arrival.

Minis were raced as soon as the first few had left the factory and obviously had to do so on the only tyre available—the standard equipment, road-going cross-ply. This was quickly strengthened and given a D7 racing tread, then a radial appeared and a ten-inch Weathermaster pattern and, in 1963, the SP3 radial. By 1964, the racing cars from Cooper and Broadspeed were chucking out 80 bhp and it was clear that there had to be far more rubber to transmit that sort of power to the road. The first real racing tyres then appeared. They were on wider rims with square shoulders which gave greater tread width on the road. They were designed to run at low pressures to get a bigger 'footprint' and the tyre walls were shallow to avoid distortion. Different tread patterns, compounds and constructions came thick and fast, and each time the tyre men thought that they had overcome the heat problem the demon engine-tuners would wring another power increase out of the cars and revive the problem all over again.

The ever-widening tyre gave rise to the spats which were riveted over the wheel arches. These were partly to reduce spray and partly to improve aerodynamics, but mostly because the Cooper Cars chief

mechanic, Ginger Devlin, had a tidy mind and would never allow his cars to be anything other than immaculate. It was his discipline that spawned the craze among Mini owners for wheel-spacers and spats, which they fitted regardless of whether or not their tyres were oversize.

Regulations prevented the racing tyres going beyond a certain width and seven inches was the greatest width for a rim ever achieved, except for some of the later super-saloons where there was no such restriction. By 1967, Minis were racing on miniature Formula One tyres, which were further refined by using an asymmetrical design. These were sharp outside shoulders with a very round inside shoulder, needed to prevent excessive inside wear while accelerating down the straight. Most drivers were specifying a very sticky compound at the front with a harder one at the rear to provoke the tail-out attitude.

The final development was the change to twelve-inch-diameter rims, made possible by reducing, by one inch, the height of the tyre sidewalls. It was quicker, ran cooler and was capable of taking softer compounds because the basic structure was more stable.

Throughout the period of development, which lasted for ten years to the end of the 1969 season, Dunlop was spurred on by two things. One was the fact that Firestone dearly wanted the contract with Cooper Cars. The other was that BMC was determined that the Ford Anglias should be kept at bay. The latter spur was removed in 1969, when the competitions department was closed by Lord Stokes after he had

All locked up and nowhere to go. Rhodes on his way to a meeting with the earth bank at Silverstone after puncturing the nearside front tyre at 100 mph. The tyres on this racing Cooper S were still quite 'thin'

acquired control under the Leyland/BMH merger. Development virtually ceased and the tyres available commercially today, to Mini competitors, have changed little since those halcyon days of rapid-fire technical improvements.

It is a happy coincidence that work began on the world's first successful small automatic gearbox at almost the same time as Issigonis started to worry about the Mini; but it was nearly ten years before the mating took place in 1965. And just as the Mini needed the discovery of the constant-velocity joint to provide the missing link, the Automotive Products four-speed gearbox was dependent on the Irish engineer Mr Hugh Reid and his bevel gear device.

Early studies at the Leamington Spa group headquarters centred around spur gear layshaft boxes with multiple clutches providing power shifts between ratios. A torque converter had been designed—as this was the only practical way of linking power source and gearbox—and it was at this point in 1956 that Mr Reid arrived. He had actually engineered the device as an overdrive unit, but it was perfectly acceptable for its new role.

The first application was as a two-speed. The Reid cluster of bevels was married to the AP torque converter and fitted to a Humber Hawk, which proceeded to give 20,000 trouble-free miles but without a reverse gear. Things became far more complicated when the next step was

A special saloon class Mini with huge wheel arches to cover the oversize racing slicks

taken—to three speeds. Two examples were fitted to Austin A50
Cambridge saloons and one of them was converted in such a way as to
ensure that the oil in the automatic box also circulated around the engine.
This gave valuable advance information on the behaviour of automatics
running in lubricant contaminated by products of combustion and other
foreign matter. It was at the height of this test work that the Mini was
announced and provided the sort of challenge that the AP engineers
could not ignore.

Two development engineers, Fred Ellis and Alan Aitkin, were
responsible for most of the development work which created a three-
speed box little larger than the standard Mini gearbox and could be fitted
in the same space beneath the engine. In April of 1962, AP's Mervyn
Cutler took the plunge and showed the work to Issigonis, who was
instantly impressed. The go-ahead was given to develop the box
specifically for the Mini, an idea which appealed to AP because it meant
that it could build up production slowly for a specific model. It also
presented the opportunity to develop the device for a fairly wide range of
applications—from Mokes to Coopers.

Almost at once it was discovered by the engineers that four speeds
could be had almost as cheaply as three, and Issigonis was even more
pleased. Slightly startled by their own success—creating four forward
gears and one reverse with only eight gear wheels—the engineers toyed
with the idea of a five-speed, but decided against the further refinement.
For years after it was launched, it remained the only box in the world
which was suitable for cars under 1300 cc in capacity and had four speeds
selected automatically or at will.

Tooling up cost AP £1 million. It used factory space at Leamington,
having shunted filter manufacture off to another facility in Bolton. In the
record time of twelve months, BMC transformed a bare machine-store in
Kings Norton, Birmingham, into a modern assembly shop where engines
and automatic gearboxes were mated. Everything was done in near-
sterile conditions. Smoking was banned and all the components were
delivered from AP individually wrapped. The cost of the assembly shop
was a further £750,000 at 1964 prices. The only components not made by
AP were the light-alloy transmission case and the bevel train gear and
final drive, which BMC's transmissions division made. Soon after
opening, the production for Mini and 1100 cars rose to 1000 units a week.

In place of the normal clutch, a torque converter is bolted to the end of
the crankshaft, and drive is then transmitted by primary gears to the main
bevel gear train in the transmission case. This is best described as a
differential within a differential. By holding different parts of the
assembly through servo-operated brake bands, the different ratios are
obtained. Two clutches are used to complete the power transmission.
One is for all forward gears, supplemented by the second when top gear
comes into use.

The second clutch also transmits reverse. The clutches drive on to the
differential, and conventional driveshafts then take the power to the road-
wheels. An oil pressure system operates the brake bands and clutches,
which are controlled by cable-operated valves from the gear-shift in the

car. The main oil pump runs with the engine, circulating oil to the torque converter and valve block as well as the engine. An extension of the throttle linkage provides additional bias for the governor and gives extra speed in the gears for accelerating as well as kick-down gear-changing.

This last refinement means that the car will even respond to the driver's subconscious. When he finds himself in a tight spot and he wants to escape rapidly, his first instinct is to floor the throttle. This will be interpreted by the governor as a change-down to the gear most suitable for maximum acceleration. Easing the throttle back will restore the cruising gear. Otherwise, the driver just sticks the control in the sector of the control quadrant marked D, and pootles around without giving it another thought and with the left leg completely rested. Or if selection of a gear manually inspires more confidence, that is equally acceptable to the automatic box.

The disadvantage of the automatic—apart from the additional purchase price—is the power loss through the torque converter partly improved by a larger carburetter. Generally assessed as being about ten per cent, this affects top speed and fuel consumption by about the same proportion. With the selector of a Mini 1000 Automatic in D, the road speeds at the point of gear change should be as follows:

On a light throttle: 11, 16, 21 mph (18, 26, 34 kph)
Full throttle: 28, 42, 54 mph (45, 67, 88 kph)
Kick-down speeds at which change-down occurs:
   Below: 43, 35, 22 mph (70, 56, 36 kph)
Over-run, throttle closed, change-down: 18, 12, 6 mph (29, 19, 9 kph)

Bernard Ferriman of Oxford believes this is the oldest Mini still in everyday service. He should know. For 20 years he ran the records department for Experimental and Research at Cowley. 434 NWL was pressed into service in June of 1959. He bought it from the test fleet three years later having converted it to right hand drive. The picture was taken in 1975. By 1984, 82 year-old Mr. Ferriman had clocked up 90,000 miles with his collectors' piece

8 Derivatives—van, pick-up and Moke

Right from the start it was realized that a car with all its vital components at the front had great versatility in spawning derivatives. You could do virtually anything you liked at the back. All the initial development work was directed at the saloon car, but as soon as that was out of the assembly hall door, work began on developing the important alternatives. Within five months, the van was on the market, and within twelve, the wood-framed estate arrived. Unlike the Morris Minor Traveller, the ash frame had no structural importance. It was there only to suggest that the Mini might be acceptable to the landed gentry. By January of 1961, the little Mini Pick-up was available and in October that year two major things happened.

One was the start of something great—the first Mini Cooper with twin carbs, disc brakes and a 997 cc engine. The other was the short-lived attempt at up-marketing—the introduction of the Riley Elf and the Wolseley Hornet.

Dick Burzi, son of an Italian father and Argentinian mother, did the work. He was discovered by Lord Austin in the nineteen-forties and invited to build dignity into the ubiquitous Mini, and, by styling a classic upright radiator at the front, veneered dash and big boot, he met his brief. The marketing men were pleased at having something new. The engineers—Issigonis included—were contemptuous. The complaint was that the cars put on weight without commensurate power increases. That criticism was dealt with within the year when what was to be the 998 cc Cooper engine was detuned with a single carburetter and made the standard equipment of the Elf and Hornet. It was such a successful pairing that on economy events which required some high-speed driving, like the Mobil Economy Drive, the Elf/Hornet was found to be more economical than the standard 850 cc Mini. It was to be another five years however before the 998 was to appear in the basic Mini, as the Mini 1000. The cylinder sizes were a bit of a cocktail. The stroke at 76.2 mm was

The early Mini estate. This one is the Austin Mini Countryman. The wood was not structural and was relatively expensive

identical to that of the discontinued Morris 1000, while the bore was the 64.6 mm of the Austin/Morris 1100. New pistons gave a compression ratio of 8.3 : 1 and power was 38 bhp.

The first major update came in 1964, almost exactly five years after the launch. What was important was that Issigonis had finally got his way with Hydrolastic suspension. It was to have a life of only seven years because, although it did civilize the ride, it was very expensive. Soon after the Leyland/BMC merger, it was dropped as an economy measure. In some markets, like Germany, where there were stringent lighting regulations, it was illegal because the car, when fully laden, sent its dipped headlights searching skywards. As the car had not been devised to accept Hydrolastic originally, engineering the pipework in such a way as to prevent chafing and impact damage was difficult and costly. But it caused no major problems in service. At the time of the announcement of Hydrolastic, BMC was enjoying the welcome the system had received when it was used in the Austin/Morris 1100 range, which was launched two years previously. It was presented as overcoming the two problems of constant attention required by conventional shock-absorbers, and variation of ride, caused by temperature, with the all-rubber suspension. The virtue of Hydrolastic is the pitch control by a fluid connection between the front and rear suspensions, along both sides of the car. Each Hydrolastic unit is a cylinder with its lower end closed by a rubber spring. Halfway up the cylinder is a partition that locates a damper valve. In the middle of the lower rubber spring is an orifice leading to a pipe which connects with the other Hydrolastic unit on the same side of the car. The whole system is filled with water treated with anti-freeze and anti-corrosion additives.

When the front wheel goes over a bump it acts against the lower diaphragm to force the water through the damper valve, which damps the shock and lifts the lower rubber spring to bring that into play also. Some of the fluid is forced down the interconnecting pipe and lifts the rear suspension slightly, thereby levelling the car and theoretically giving a pitch-free ride. The development problem was that the so-called wet springs had to be interchangeable with the dry springs of the Mini. These were 5.25 inches in diameter, a size which caused very high loading on the diaphragm and a degree of unreliability, and Dunlop, who made them, and Alex Moulton, who designed them, had to work very hard to get them into production by October 1964.

Paddy Hopkirk was once quoted as saying that Hydrolastic suspension was worth ten seconds a mile, but then as a BMC employee he could hardly be expected to say that BMC's latest joy was a retrograde step. Mini enthusiasts were unconvinced about the benefits. The system lost pressure easily and left the body hanging perilously close to the bump-stops, and it did little to improve the inherent problem of the 'dry' Mini,

The assault that killed the AA salute. In 1967 they left their motorcycle combinations en masse to go under cover with vans. The Mini van was the ideal answer

which was jerkiness of ride. The front of the Hydrolastic car drooped, and rose and fell through about three inches when accelerated or braked hard. Rally enthusiasts found that by careful throttle control they could lift the front end over bumps. But most preferred to swap the units for competition displacers, which were only four per cent dearer, for they restored the car to its normal height, eradicated the rise and fall and improved the roll. The only problem was that they were so stiff that they inflicted great punishment on the body, which would age prematurely and acquire all sorts of unfamiliar creaks and groans.

An artist's airbrush impression
of the Mini Pick-up

A major scare in 1965 brought the whole of BMC engineering to a virtual standstill for several weeks. A metallurgist by the name of Professor Derry, was convinced that constant-velocity joints were breaking and causing accidents. Charles Griffin was assigned the task of soothing the public outcry and for five weeks he was on call for just about every coroner in the land. The constant-velocity joint was badly misunderstood and to assist the Ministry of Transport inspector, Griffin stocked a large box with samples of every kind of breakage possible. It gave the inspectors a point of reference by which they could define the problem in their own particular case. Griffin himself was touring the country giving evidence at inquests with the burden of proving that the joints were breaking *in* the accidents and not before them. The point was finally made at an inquest in Eccles, Lancashire, and just to make sure it was shown that even if a half-shaft did break, it could not constitute an accident danger. His travelling companion for the traumatic tour of the coroners' courts was Bill Cull. Cull was the man who sorted out the constant-velocity joint with Hardy Spicer and who ensured that front-wheel drive as a means of mass transportation became a reality. Front-wheel drive had, of course, been possible for many years. Citroën was quite happily using a double Hooke's joint, but it was a system that did not miniaturize well and which was not cheap and easy to make. The fear that the constant-velocity joints were causing injury was real but unjustified.

Far more serious was a feature on the car which went unnoticed for six years. It was not until January 1966 that safety bosses were fitted under the leading edge of the lever-action door handles. Nobody had demanded the change, but for one Solihull boy it came too late. By a freak

The Riley Elf had a code name of Riley 8 and in its original state, white-wall tyres. This is a prototype of late 1960

chance, the forward-facing handle caught him under the rib-cage as a car passed him in the street.

The Mark II arrived in October 1967. The Elf 998 cc engine was introduced in a new model known as the 1000 Super de-luxe alongside the 850 cc car. All models had a two-inch wider rear window, larger front grille, new badging and interior seats and trim. The chrome framing of the front grille was bolder and larger tail lamps were fitted to meet certain foreign requirements. This caused the small auxiliary bumper rails, which were a sign of the better specification, to be discontinued because they got in the way. The Mark II solved some of the niggly problems. Use of seat belts had been growing since legislation made their fitment compulsory, but once strapped in to a static belt, only drivers with the proportions of a gorilla could reach the switches on the centre fascia. Mark II modifications brought the switches three inches nearer the driver. Owners had also found it frustrating to own a small car that had a poor turning circle—thirty-one feet. This was remedied with a twenty-five tooth steering rack instead of a fifteen and longer steering arms. The circle is now twenty-eight feet. Brake action was improved with twin leading shoe front brakes.

It was in 1969 that the outline of the Mini was defiled by the Clubman front. American Filmer Paradise, the sales director of the day, wanted the car to have a more up-market appeal in order to lift the prices, and the man who met the brief was Roy Haynes, who had been recruited from Ford. Throughout the late nineteen-sixties, Haynes was being pushed by managing director Joe Edwards to come up with a completely new body

The Hydrolastic system at the front. The suspension arrangement lasted for seven years only, from 1964 to 1971

The boss that was fitted for safety reasons at the leading edge of the door handle in 1966

for the Mini. The drawings that emerged were no great improvement and plans to relaunch the car were shelved. The halfway-house of the Clubman front was adopted instead. To the engineer it was the greatest horror so far. It did increase the usefulness of the under-bonnet space a little but increased the drag of the car and the fuel consumption.

Coincidental to the introduction of the Clubman was the extensive revision of the short-nosed car. Apart from the discontinuation of Hydrolastic on the 850 and 1000, the new car (coded ADO 20) had

'It takes one to catch one' department. Some police forces used Mk II Cooper S patrol cars

negative earth, mechanical fuel pump and concealed door hinges instead of the rust-prone external devices. Most significant of all was the adoption of the wind-up window. It was a rather sad move, for it marked a loss of courage by BMC management and a trend towards conformity. The original Mini design was stuffed full of space-saving ideas and stowage areas. Drop-windows lost the capacious stowage bins on the doors and nearly five inches of elbow room. At the same time, the estate car became available only with a Clubman front—the one application which retained some sort of styling balance—and the Cooper was dropped in favour of the 1275GT. Just to complete the clean sweep in 1969, the Elf and Hornet went to that great car park in the sky. Of all the Mini derivatives, the shortest-lived on the British market was the Moke. It was only four when it was transported to Australia in 1968, for assembly there.

The Mini Moke started life as a stab at a military application. The concept was right because every armed force in the world wanted a vehicle sturdy enough to withstand a parachute drop, light enough to be lifted by a small helicopter, and which could be packed flat and stored one on top of another. But it was the lack of ground clearance that made it impractical, so the Moke had to stand or fall by its acceptability as a fun vehicle.

Customs and Excise soul-searched for ages, but eventually dealt it a mortal blow by deciding that it was not a commercial vehicle and should carry Purchase Tax. The specialists seized on it as a base for an open-air taxi in parts of the world where the weather could be guaranteed, and the rich and famous throughout the world hankered after a version which was converted as a golf caddy.

It was Issigonis who first spotted the idea of putting an engine at the back as well as the front. Early in 1963, he called John Cooper down to see him at Longbridge to inspect his 'new toy'. From out of a garage was wheeled a Moke with a 950 cc engine forward and an 850 aft. John Cooper drove it through the thick snow for which that winter was infamous and found that he could 'drive as fast as he could see'.

In February, the Press was invited along to watch the curiosity in action on the lawn at Longbridge. Just to prove that it could have some uses, it was laden with hay bales to haul through the snow. The idea for the next logical step struck Cooper and Issigonis simultaneously on that day, and they rushed off to their respective workshops to set wheels in motion. Cooper won by a day and within a matter of weeks had got his Twini Mini saloon to the point where it was worth track testing. John Whitmore took the car—which with an engine on the back seat sounded like an American dragster—to Brands Hatch.

He found that with two engines there was sufficient power to actually haul the car out of the bends—something that could never be done with the standard car. By April, both engines were fully-tuned Coopers and the result was a 2.5-litre vehicle developing 175 bhp, and wheelspin on all four wheels.

In August, BMC asked Downton Engineering to prepare a Twini for the classic Sicilian road race—the Targa Florio. Apart from one four-mile straight, the forty-four-mile circuit is an endless struggle for the driver, through narrow mountain passes where often there is insufficient room for two cars to pass. The drivers were John Whitmore and Paul Frère, the Belgian journalist and grand prix driver. Another team of Rob Slotemaker and Bernard Cahier was assigned a 1200 cc Downton mono Mini. The crews spent three days on a recce of the course, and after twenty laps two Alfas, a Fiat and a Morris Oxford later thought that they had a grasp of 700 of the corners. In official practice, the Twini Mini managed a lap time of 47 minutes 11 seconds—including a spin on a wet patch beneath trees—and the mono Mini did a fifty-minute lap in the hands of both its drivers. At its fastest speed, the Twini was getting through a set of tyres every two laps, so it was decided to go for a lap time of fifty minutes.

In the race, both cars were troubled with water loss. The mono changed water and drivers every lap, while the Twini burst its rear radiator on the start line but lost coolant at a slightly slower rate. Paul Frère opened the account with three fifty-six-minute laps out of deference to the water problems. Daniel Richmond of Downton made a determined effort to fix the leak after the fourth lap, when Whitmore turned in a scorching forty-nine. In a bid to make up time, he did a forty-eight on the next lap, and when he approached the pits, the temperature of the rear engine was reading normal, so he swept by. But only a mile later, all the water had gone and the rear engine had to be disconnected. Thereafter, the car lapped in an uncompetitive fifty-five against the steady average of fifty-one by the mono. The winner of the race was the Bonnier and Abate Porsche, which picked up the lead a mile from the finish when a Ferrari crashed.

Nothing went untried in forming the Mini family, even if there was clearly no market for them in Britain. Quite a few beach cars were built by specialists for overseas orders, mainly for hotel courtesy fleets

Another beach car prototype using some odd styling tricks

128

The first Twini Moke on test in February 1963 on the Longbridge lawn. The hay bales were to show that the Twini could be useful for something

Opposite, above A backward Moke is rushed up a slope by a keen Australian demonstration driver

Opposite Pack-flat Mokes. The canvas tilts were despatched in the boxes

Failure seemed to dog the tracks of the Twini and enthusiasm was even further dampened when John Cooper had a horrific accident in a road-going Twini. It was the third in a series of accidents in which Cooper was involved and very nearly the last. He was returning from Fairoaks airport having been to collect his Tri-pacer light aircraft. This had crashed some months earlier when he and Lotus chief Colin Chapman were aboard with a professional pilot at the controls. It had cartwheeled on landing without causing injury to anyone. When he collected it, it had sustained further damage while on the ground. The tailplane was badly bent and had he failed to notice it before trying to take off, he could have been in serious trouble again. As it was, he was in a hurry on his way home to collect his wife, Paula, at Surbiton to join Salvadori for dinner.

The Twini was equipped with two 1300 cc engines, which were to have been tweaked up to 135 bhp apiece with fuel injection. Batting along the Kingston bypass at 100 mph, the steering arm that had been welded-up to the rear subframe came adrift. As the rack had been removed, the steering link had been used as a suspension arm. The wheel was suddenly free and made a sharp right turn. The car catapulted end-over-end into a wall, throwing Cooper clear but fracturing his skull. Few who saw him thought he would live. The first car on the scene—one that Cooper had just overtaken—contained a lady who suffered a nervous breakdown as a result of seeing the accident unfold, and she tried unsuccessfully to claim for compensation from Cooper's insurance.

The headache lasted Cooper a lifetime, but his personal conviction that Twinis were winners never disappeared. He was convinced they

Top The Twini Moke with two 1100 cc engines was sent to America for US Army evaluation. Nothing ever resulted from it

Above Twini Mini built at Longbridge for the 1963 Targa Florio. Charles Griffin was due to drive it but was forbidden from so doing by George Harriman because of the risks involved

Top Australian-built Mini Moke turned flat-bed truck

Above This special Australian-built Moke tackled the London to Sydney Rally in 1977 in the hands of Hans Tholstrup. The kangaroo bars were an essential, as encounters with the wildlife were frequent

were cheaper than four-wheel-drive transmission systems and was sure that for hazardous missions in snow or mud, an armed force could gain a lot from carrying a 'spare engine'. On a flat road, either the front or rear engine could be run singly as preferred by the driver.

Two successful Mini club racers took up the challenge in 1964—more determined to do something different than to make the Twini work. Gordon Allen was the pioneering designer and Rod Embley his nominated driver. Allen has a history of special engines and for the 1963 season had been running a Mini with a 1500 cc Ford engine. The extra weight over the front wheels had created massive understeer. For the Twini project, he designed his own aluminium block and adapted Jaguar heads. The first results were track-burning acceleration and even worse understeer than before. The prospect that worried Embley was that if one engine was to miss a beat, the characteristics of the handling would suddenly change and make an accident inevitable.

Embley said after his first encounter at Silverstone: 'The road-holding was not good by mono Mini standards, but after what people had talked me into expecting I was very pleasantly surprised. The rear engine, in fact, increased the understeer and at no stage was there a transition from understeer to oversteer, however hard I accelerated with both throttles together. By cornering on medium front-engine throttle and increasing the rear, understeer could gradually be transformed to oversteer. But I found that the usefulness of this correction depended on the radius of the curve and could best be used on a medium fast corner like Copse corner. Acceleration was quite fantastic, the gear-change surprisingly good and positive, and the noise-levels inside quite insane—which was not surprising with two Webers within a couple of feet of my ear.'

The car could not be hurled about like a normal saloon and was, therefore, at some disadvantage in traffic on a tightly packed circuit or when trying to negotiate a way through back markers. Braking—which was weak anyway—was very dicy unless all four wheels lay in the same plane. The special engines caused all sorts of protests from other Mini racers—not least on the grounds that there was no back seat, therefore it did not qualify as a saloon!

9 Pre-production and post-production cars

Sir Leonard Lord did not put all his eggs into Issigonis's basket when he wanted a new car; he also placed a development contract with ERA at Dunstable. ERA was the racing car company founded by Raymond Mays making 1.5 and 2-litre racing cars which dominated some road racing, just pre- and post-war. (Its engineers also contributed to the Jowett Jupiter sports car.) In 1956, when Issigonis moved into the inner sanctum at Longbridge, David Hodkin at ERA was invited to start work with a similar design brief. Laurence Pomeroy, technical editor of *Motor* magazine, was commissioned to act as the ideas man for Hodkin and for him it was a difficult time. He was a good friend to Issigonis, but was under instructions not to discuss ideas with him so that there would be no duplication of development. He and Hodkin came up with a rear-engined, air-cooled car code-named Maximin, which had the engine cast in aluminium and mounted transversely between the rear wheel-arches. Suspension was on Firestone air-bags with a constant-height regulator. A conventional gearbox had automatic shifts at fixed engine speeds. Although the short-lived NSU 1000 used precisely this engine layout, it was considered too complex and attracted little support. The car stood at Longbridge for some time before it was disposed of.

At Cowley there was another project being run by ex-Wolseley man Charles Griffin, with Bob Shirley and Reg Job. They were aiming at a target set by the BMC technical director, Sidney Smith, who wanted a car costing no more than £300 to build. They actually succeeded, while Issigonis failed by some £15 or £20. It was built round the two-cylinder version of the A-series engine which Issigonis also played with briefly. The engine was mounted transversely ahead of the rear axle and the body was designed around the idea of a high sill and a sliding canopy.

It was one of two 'rival' projects for which Griffin was responsible, even though he was a key member of the Issigonis team. For just before the Mini went into production, the engineers decided to put themselves

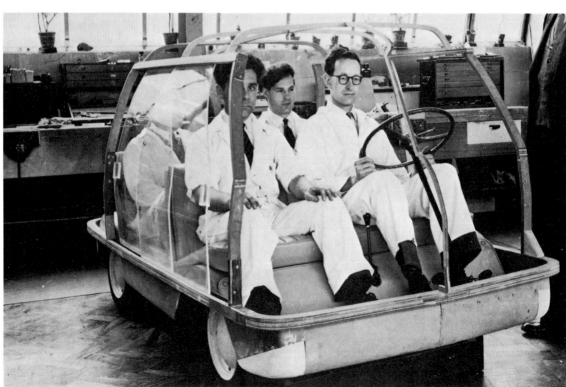

DO 19. The damning feature was that the feet of the front seat occupants would have been far too near the accident

Opposite A derivative that would have pleased many a young Mum—a long wheel-base Mini with four doors

in the minds of their competitors and see if they could execute a rear-wheel-drive car with space utilization as good as the Mini's. Called DO 19, it had adjustable rear seats so that emphasis could be given to legroom or luggage space. It was a one-box car like the Fiats of the day, but not quite so van-like. With the engine at the back, the space utilization *was* better, but it was decided totally unusable because, as Griffin put it, the driver's feet were too near the accident.

The Mini came nearest to being replaced in 1976, and had it not been for the constant changes in management and policies, the plan would have gone through. The proposal had been created in Advanced Engineering at Longbridge and accepted for production with only two changes to the specification finalized by the then director of advanced engineering, Charles Griffin. The ADO 88 project was not a radical rethink of the existing Mini. It simply set out to correct what was wrong with the existing car. Had it gone through on the original time-scale, it would have been available for public inspection at the first International Motor Show held at the National Exhibition Centre in Birmingham in 1978.

The three major faults that Griffin sought to improve were noise, ride and erosion of width. First he corrected what he saw as the schoolboy error of building a car with two inches narrower track at the rear than the front, which with no gain in overall dimensions lost two inches from the back seat. Then he widened the external width by two inches. The sides of the car were curved to put back all the elbow-room that was lost when the drop-windows became a standard feature, and the car was made longer to follow the theory that there was no longer any advantage in being ultra-small. Inside, the gains in width were six and a half inches at the front and eight and a half at the back. Styling was by Harris Mann, the designer of both the Princess 1800/2200 and the TR7. The lines, therefore, gave a hint of the wedge shape which was beginning to outline the family connection in the Leyland range. Not too wedgy because of the high bonnet necessary to envelop an engine over a gearbox, but wedgy enough to incorporate the known benefits in accidents with pedestrians and to allow a bumper height that standardized with international regulations. The length was ten feet six inches and the body low-drag with a coefficient of 0·4. There was the obligatory hatchback, lateral rear lights and curved side glasses.

Experience under Harry Webster, when a Mini was built six inches wider than normal, showed that weight went up nineteen pounds for every extra inch in width. Extra length by contrast—and leg-room is generally the criterion for comfort—is only twelve pounds an inch unless the work is performed on the under-bonnet structures, in which case it is halved to six pounds an inch. The Griffin project was very much feet-on-the-ground. His philosophy was to get on and develop what the company already had on the shelf rather than 'baying at the moon'. He believed that the cardinal sin of the engineering department over the years was not spending enough time working on its own creations. Hydrolastic and Hydragas both have great intrinsic merit and Griffin believed that with the proper development they could have kept Leyland

137

Dick Burzi doodles for styling changes

The barrel phase. It was thought possible to increase interior space significantly without changing the identity. The clay buck shows the curved side glasses and a bonnet with raised edges—reminiscent of the style used by both Simca and Peugeot

The barrel phase with a new bonnet. The grille style was clearly chosen to give a family resemblance to the 1800 series

The back of the barrel. In addition to the curved sides, the rear view shows the removal of the flanges

Bespectacled Dick Burzi discusses the finer points of 9X with chief designer of cars, 'Ben' Benbow. The car was put together under Issigonis in 1968 by a team led by John Sheppard

The rear of 9X showing the half-hatch rear door. The car was several years ahead of its time and superior to the later Innocenti three-door Mini. The number of parts involved in production would have been reduced by forty-two per cent compared with the conventional Mini

The Innocenti operation in Milan, Italy, added to its famous Lambretta scooter operations in 1961 by making Austins under licence. It decided to try Minis in 1965 even though it meant selling them for twelve per cent more than the Fiat 850, and it proved a hit. British Leyland took direct control in 1972 when it introduced the Cooper 1300 (with 1275 S engine). When the Cooper agreement expired in 1974, BL introduced the Bertone-bodied Innocenti Mini 120 and Mini 90.

The interior of the Mini 120 which British drivers were destined never to see.
All hopes of a British launch were buried when BL pulled out of Innocenti because of mounting losses, retaining some control of vehicle distribution in Europe but leaving the entrepreneur Alexandro de Tomaso to run manufacture. As his name was already associated with sports cars, he restyled the Innocenti slightly and gave it a de Tomaso identification bank along the flank. Many were red in colour and inevitably dubbed Tomatoes

The 1000 cc Mini 90 (the hieroglyphics on the number plate read Mini) arrived at the same time as the 120.
Body panels for the two cars were stamped in Birmingham and shipped in kits with the rest of the Mini mechanical parts. Because of the hatchback fashion, many observers suggested that introduction of the Innocenti to Britain would cure Leyland's problem in the small car market and at one stage a 5,000-cars-a-year programme was planned but never implemented.
The Innocenti provided new style and a rear door without solving the problems of noise and ride. In addition it had its own problems of lack of rigidity, insufficient rear-seat head-room and expensive construction

as far ahead of the field in the nineteen-eighties as they did in the nineteen-sixties, when Ford was still side-valve and three-speed.

Griffin did not share the view that sub-frames made the Mini critically expensive to build. He saw them as an essential element of the endeavour to sophisticate small cars. 'Jaguars have sub-frames and they are the quietest and most refined cars in the world. They are a great benefit in noise suppression and we should be making them better rather than copying the competition. That is the expensive route to mediocrity.' He believed that taking the sub-frames out of the Mini involved as much piece-cost as leaving them in. He had ideas for the suspension as well, ideas which would more closely integrate suspension, structure and shock absorption.

In 1977, Alex Park, the British Leyland managing director, selected by Lord Ryder after the Ryder report, and his Leyland Cars managing director, Derek Whittaker, decided that the Griffin route might be a

Top A Mini Special 1100 built in Seneffe, Belgium, for all European markets in 1975

Above Glass-fibre body. The change from metal was to create an assembly operation in Chile, where there was no metal-pressing facility. The only way to make use of the required amount of local labour was to organize manufacture of glass-fibre shells. The absence of the external flanges creates quite a difference in appearance. (Racing enthusiasts often removed the flanges in order to save over forty square inches of frontal area.) Ironically it was because it was envisaged that the Mini would be built around the world by unskilled labour that the external flanges were designed in the first place. They were thought likely to make things easier for the unskilled welder. It was also thought that manufacture in Britain could be done more cheaply by employing cheaper unskilled labour but the unions would have none of it and another BMC cost-cutting idea bit the dust

From the world of Roy Haynes—the hump-backed Mini

mistake and that what was needed was a car capable of taking on the second generation super-Minis which were appearing all over the world. When these two executives were overthrown by Michael Edwardes, there was a brief pause for an inquest. Edwardes came down in favour of what went before and he appointed Ray Horrocks—the man who had built up the advanced vehicle operation for Ford—to the job of controlling the future of Austin/Morris and the Mini.

By October 1978 the specification of the Metro was frozen and the company threw its whole weight behind getting it into production within eighteen months. It was code-named LC8—accurately reflecting kinship with ADO 88. The major difference between the two cars was size.

The aim, as always with Austin Morris, was to get the maximum internal dimensions from the minimum overall dimensions, to package the car so that there was an infinite number of specifications from the lowly to the lavish and to give versatility. The shape was a compromise between a hatchback and a conventional boot to appeal to both schools of thought.

The cost of getting the new car ready was estimated at about £300 million and included building a huge new body shop on the Longbridge site. Everyone on the company knew that this was the last chance for Austin Morris. If LC8 was not produced efficiently, and in quantity, if it was not right first time and misfired with the motorists, there would be no more Austin Morris. For there is a limit to the number of Government rescues any one company can have.

Between the Haynes designs and the abortive ADO 88 project there were other phases of development which could have resulted in the Mini being reclothed. In 1970 Rob Owen, a styling engineer at Longbridge, drove a standard Mini 1275GT to Italy, where for two months he supervised a project at Michelotti. When the new stylish bodyshell had been built on to the 1275GT platform, Owen drove it back to Longbridge. It was considered the basis of a replacement for the MG Midget, looking rather fetching with its two-seater cabin and large top panels for stowing in the boot. Because it was hand-built it was rather heavy, but apart from twin tailpipes the specification was identical to that of the saloon and it was therefore slower.

There was a strong body of opinion in Longbridge that sports car enthusiasts did not want front-wheel drive. The real sports car is the one which can be steered at both ends; one with the steering wheel and the other with the throttle. But it was not this that killed the car, the problem was much more straightforward. America was the single most important market for British sports cars, and to get there engines had to meet rigorous emission standards. The cost of detoxing the GT engine was to be prohibitive, so instead the MG Midget was equipped with the instantly available Triumph Spitfire engine and the Michelotti project was shelved.

There were two other attempts at a sports car that got as far as running prototypes. Longbridge produced a 2+2 coupé in 1964 which looked pretty terrible and would have needed the Farina treatment even for presentation to senior management. It had no panels common with the

This is a heavily camouflaged ADO 88 during the period immediately prior to the changeover to the LC8 concept which became Metro

Mini saloon and would have been a pure extravagance.

An open four-seater was produced independently at Abingdon using the longer floor-pan of the Minivan as a basis. Again, there were no common panels. As the specialist manufacturers have shown time and again, it is almost impossible to achieve elegance and a sense of proportion in a Mini-sized sports car. The factory attempts had no greater success.

Issigonis thought that the most important refinement for the Mini was a new engine and he played with just about every conceivable option. The reason that he never got any of them into production was simple. It would have cost tens of millions of pounds to write off the tooling for the A-series engine and the corporation's continual financial crises never allowed that luxury.

Most refined of all the refinements was a six-cylinder engine. It was lovely to drive behind, but the arguments which raged about fuel

The Clubman front was beginning to emerge as a fixed idea, but with only seventeen months to go before the launch of the car, chief stylist Haynes was still intent on providing a bigger boot, even to the extent of staging a revival of the Riley Elf back-end

Tidy and stylish, the Michelotti Mini would have ousted the MG Midget had it got the green light

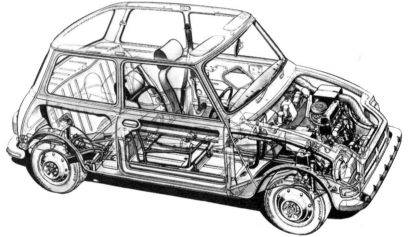

Top On the *left*, the standard 1275GT, and on the *right* the version for a man and wife and their elbows. Eight inches went into the width and everything else stayed the same. The idea was tried in 1973 but the economics of increasing width were prohibitive and the car got no further than the factory vehicle pool

Leyland's Experimental Safety Vehicle showing increased impact protection, with drooping front end to scoop pedestrians on to the bonnet rather than knocking them flat, and lower bumper heights

economy became endless. How could an engine with more friction to overcome be ultimately more economic than a four-cylinder?

At the National Engineering Laboratory in East Kilbride, a joint project was run which attempted ultimate efficiency by running a Mini with a hydraulic motor on each of the wheels. It was always defeated by unacceptably high noise-levels.

Issigonis experimented for two years with a steam engine, and the Mini was even subjected to a gas turbine implant in a project that ran in parallel with the gas-turbine Rover. It was rear-engined but still front-wheel drive.

The project that engrossed Issigonis totally in the late nineteen-seventies was the idea of stepless and fully automatic transmission. His own blue Mini has a surreal appearance from the driver's seat, for there is no gear lever at all—not even the little automatic shift. His ambition had always been to create a simple system that was as cheap or cheaper than the manual gearbox and just as reliable. The Hobbs Variable Kinetic Drive gave the same effect but was far too complex for Issigonis.

Soon after Michael Edwardes became Chairman of British Leyland in

145

DAE 137C

During the 1973 petrol crisis, the Electricity Council loaned its experimental battery-powered Mini Traveller to Geoffrey Rippon, Secretary of the Environment. It was capable of 40 mph and would travel twenty-five miles after charging for four hours

1977, he went to meet Issigonis at his home and told him that he needed something new and revolutionary for the small car. Issigonis not only impressed the virtues of stepless transmission upon him, but lent him the car, which Edwardes and his wife used in London for a month. But nothing came of the encounter.

In one experiment, the automatic system was linked up to the 1750 cc E-series (Maxi) engine in a Mini (it will fit almost anywhere the A-series engine will go). The prototype was estimated to be 150 lb. overweight, but accelerated from rest to 106 mph in one gear. The project fascinated Issigonis in his semi-retirement because the research involved the whole car. He had never been involved in researching just parts of a car as is the modern design discipline, and he never had any intention of being just part of a team.

His last complete car project was the 9X, a car which very nearly went into production but was caught by the BMH/Leyland merger. Development was in full swing at the same time as Haynes was perfecting the Clubman shape. The 9X was the same size as the Mini, but looked like a Ford Fiesta and weighed less than both. Suspension was conventional because, by that time, Issigonis believed that rubber was too expensive, too hard and 'settled' more than was tolerable. The front was McPherson strut and the rear trailing arms with little coil springs. The body was two inches wider — to restore some of the width lost from his original design by wind-up windows—and there was four inches more leg-room. This was achieved by using a new engine designed with the prime intention of making it narrower. It was overhead cam in both four- and six-cylinder derivatives.

Issigonis worked almost alone on the car but for the help of a small team of draughtsmen controlled by John Sheppard, and it was ready for production in 1968. Subsequently, Issigonis was glad that it was never built. As the look-alike cars arrived from all the European manufacturers, he began to see the Mini shape as an irreplaceable asset to the company. So instead, he set out to modify the existing body-shell in such a way as to accommodate all his mechanical refinements. Such huge changes were needed for the floor-pan that the research never got much further than the concept stage, and ADO 88 began to get preference.

Although it never reached the stage of a road-going prototype, ADO 74 was a very thorough project estimated in March 1974 (when it was cancelled) to cost £130 million to get into production. Work on it was going on exactly the time Ford was developing the Fiesta and had British Leyland gone ahead, the two cars would have hit the market at about the same time. It was taken sufficiently seriously for all details to have been kept a close secret until now.

The brief for the car—and the brief to which stylist Harris Mann worked—was to make something bigger than the Mini that would command a bigger price.

Its dimensions were to be 11 feet 6 inches by 5 feet $1\frac{1}{2}$ inches—larger than the LC8—with a wedge-shaped front end that was a preferred BL family styling trait.

Engineering came under Harry Webster but the major contribution, particularly on the matter of cost-effectiveness came from Tom Penny. The engine was also new and called the K-series. In April of 1972, Webster filed patents for the unit which had the advantage of a single casting in either iron or alloy for a combined cylinder block, crankcase and gearbox casing. It was the cost of such a radically new engine design combined with the price of remaking the body that made the investment untenably

Aston Martin Lagonda designer Bill Towns stole the limelight at the 1973 London Motor Show with his Minissima, a town car that was only 7 feet 6 inches in length. It had the Mini engine with automatic gearbox, two inward-facing rear seats and a turning circle of only twenty-one feet. It had only one door at the rear. As it was so short, it was possible to park at right angles to the kerb

It never got further than the concept stage but ADO 74 was Harris Mann's answer to the next generation Mini. The stylist of the Princess and TR7 sports car was called in to make the little car bigger. Marketing people wanted it bigger and the accountants wanted it bigger so that it could earn more. But Leyland International wanted the small car to retain an individual attraction in Europe and the project was shelved

expensive. Had the company known at that stage how great would become the demand for small cars, and that every other major company in the world was going to have to make profits out of front wheel drive, there might easily have been a decision to spend the £130 million.

ADO 74 was typical of the present new generation cars even to the extent of having MacPherson strut suspension. The two diagrams prepared by Webster to accompany patent applications show a schematic sectional view of a combined cylinder block, crankcase and gearbox and differential casing of the power unit and a fragmentary underside plan view of the power unit with the sump removed.

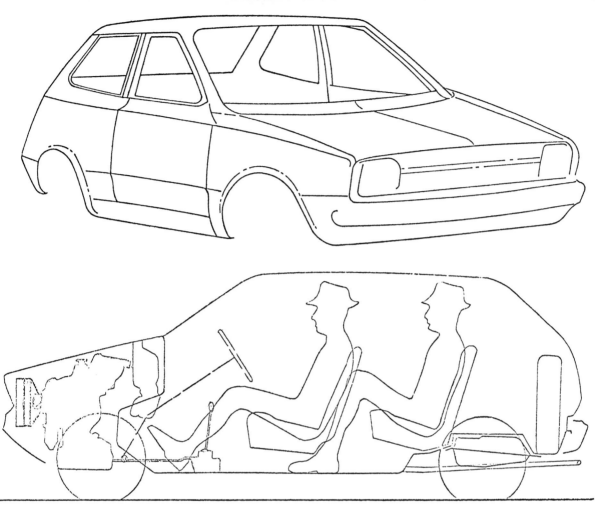

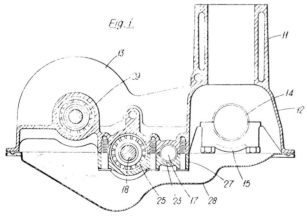

Fig. i

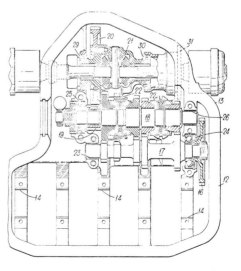

ADO 74 at the early planning stage. The top drawing gives
nothing but an impression of the shape. The second one
was labelled 'Package Configuration'. The last two show a
cross-section and sump-pan-off plan of the power-train casting

10   Arrival of the Metro

David Bache had one of the best overviews of the inside story of the Metro project's separation from Mini-replacement. As a Rover stylist he was responsible for the phenomenally successful Range Rover and subsequently for the SD1 Rover, but later he moved over from Rover with a brief to oversee the small car programme and to unify design throughout Leyland Cars.

The ADO88 design which had been under the wing of Harris Mann worried Bache—he wanted to create more 'form and interest' in the body panel. Time was short, but he thought it important to commission another five prototypes to be compared with ADO88.

The first—known as the 'evolutionary from Mini route'—was ready by November 1975. It was two inches longer than the Clubman, and had a third door and nicely rounded near end.

Pininfarina, the Italian styling house, provided the major external contribution. The association was something of a throwback as that company had been responsible for the first hatchback in Europe—the Austin A40. They were asked to come up with an 'extreme solution'—one that had heavily defined body panels and carried over the suggestion of the Mini's external welded seams.

It arrived in Britain on December 18 1975. Alan Edis, the then director of product planning, went with Bache to the airport to collect Sergio Pininfarina then went straight to the styling studio in Solihull at midnight to view the prototype.

High cost impactable pads front and rear and headlamp shapes that were very difficult to make and expensive to service, made it a rank outsider and when the Leyland board viewed the car alongside the four other new Bache commissions it was tossed out.

The board wanted to proceed with ADO88.

Bache was still worried and pressed for the car to go to a consumer clinic before any final decision was taken. It was that test that finally confirmed the worst fears in the company. The car scored a worse rating than the Ford Fiesta which had just been announced in Europe.

Bache won the day but had a new problem. The board agreed that changes had to be made but stipulated that the existing grille, bonnet, screen, roof and rear door must be maintained.

Reworked sides and interiors were sent to another clinic and came up with excellent results. On 11 January 1978 the car—by then tagged the LC8—was signed off for production.

The principal distinction had become the perceived size of the car. The back panel had been 'kinked' out to give a steeper rake to the rear screen and sharper cut off to the tail. Overall length therefore increased by two inches—improving boot space and re-emphasising that this was not a replacement for the Mini.

Although the changes were small the amount of engineering work required to get the car into production increased by 30 per cent. That meant a delay on the original timescale of nearly a year, and the convenient date of the NEC Motor Show in October 1980 was fixed as a target date.

How the TR7 designer Harris Mann saw the task of ADO88 before the arrival of Rover stylist David Bache

Right Heavily emphasized outline excused what Bache saw as lack of form in the original ADO88 study

Below This study was known as the 'evolutionary from Mini' route and built a third door into classic Mini shape

88 4 1175   REC

Below Heavy outline and emphasis on a functional character which would have meant a low showroom price

ADO88 4 1175   REC

The rest is history. Metro received a welcome better than anyone could have hoped and by 1984 was regularly ranking as the best selling car in Britain.

Minis continued to sell in such numbers that there could be no question of ending the car's run. It was getting cheaper to make because it shared Metro's production facilities in final assembly. They were a good deal more efficient than was the case when Mini was first conceived.

And the little car was not monopolising resources that would be more cost effective if they were occupied by Metro, nor was it distracting people from buying Metro.

Metro's first effect on the Mini range was for the Clubman estate body to be phased out. Austin Rover chairman, Harold Musgrove had no regrets about that.

'It was the original Mini shape that was so distinctive and which carried so much affection. The estate shape did nothing to enhance that and we were happy to phase it out and concentrate on the "mininess" of Mini.'

Legislation was the black cloud on the horizon that always seemed to be threatening Mini but the storm never broke.

This study mixed the evolutionary from Mini route and the Fiat Panda-style emphasis of functionality

It was thought that the performance of the steering wheel in an accident could outlaw it. Bumper heights were often considered by the legislators but a standard that excluded the Mini was never introduced.

And most important of all, it was thought that the external seams of the car could become illegal. Pedestrian safety required that cars should have a smooth external profile so that in a collision the pedestrian was not snagged by sharp protuberances.

That really would have been an awful blow to Mini had it happened. Stylists always agreed that it was the raised external seams that were heavily responsible for the car's individual appearance.

Engineers looked at the problem long and hard. To build the car any other way would not only affect the appearance. It would also mean a radical change to production tools. In the end they found that it would be possible to cover the seams. Unsatisfactory — but possible. Again, the legislation envisaged never arrived.

As Austin Rover began to modernise and improve its range with Metro, Maestro and Montego, the Mini came under scrutiny for another reason.

Was it an embarrassment? The reply was not long coming. In most overseas markets the Mini remained an asset. The Clubman, granted, had been a car for a particular period and was better off dead. The original Mini though retained its extraordinary mystique, its classlessness and its popularity. No question of it being an embarrassment. It was an asset to dealers.

So what could kill Mini. Musgrove again: 'Mini will come to the end of its life when it gets in the way of other cars which because of their better cost base give a better return.'

Mini was using only one line of CAB 1 and was not holding up expansion. Nor was it monopolising too much engineering and development time. Without completely redesigning the car there was no way that it could be built cheaper with fewer assembly operations. No one had ever attempted to go through those hoops. Nor would they.

After the launch of Metro, Mini went through the same facilities as its bigger brother from the paint stage to the finished car. That had meant that the 1980s cost of construction was substantially down on the 1979 cost.

Mini also shared in the general efficiency that swept through Longbridge with the arrival of the man who is now Sir Michael Edwardes.

The gross line rate efficiency in the mid-seventies could be as low as 65 per cent. By the mid-eighties that had become 95 per cent at worst.

That means that in the seventies there were 30 per cent more people on the assembly line than there should have been.

One major engineering initiative in the early eighties was taken because of the disproportionately high cost of maintaining special items for the Mini.

By 1983 it was clear that Austin Rover could no longer go on buying drum brakes for Mini alone. It had to standardise on discs which meant bigger wheels to tuck them into. So just as the 1275GT had moved onto big wheels and discs to cope with performance, the Mini City and

Mayfair moved up onto twelve inchers to stay price sensitive.

When Metro arrived and the Mini range was tailored to be complementary to it, certain assumptions were made about the way that Mini would sell. Although sales were immediately halved and there was an inevitable downward drift in the total number sold, the sales performance each and every year beat the sales assumptions.

What's more, it was found that Mini responded unfailingly to promotion. Each and every time Austin Rover thought that they might be seeing the dying breath of Mini popularity, they would put a bit of promotion behind it in terms of dealer incentives or advertising, and sales would leap back to where they were.

Assumptions were wrong too on the model mix. Planners quite reasonably assumed that there would be more takers for the Mini City that was cheaper than the Metro, than the Mini Mayfair—which was dearer.

So they proposed 60 per cent of City and 40 per cent of the plusher car. The reality was an exact turnaround.

11 Minilimmo

Peter Sellers only had to say what he wanted and Radford obliged. After the hatchback had been perfected other people wanted replicas

It was Peter Sellers who started it all with his much publicized Mini that had wickerwork panels on the doors. The work was done for him through H. R. Owen by Hooper, one of the most famous coachbuilders of all time, whose Rolls-Royce bodies are considered by some to be the very best. Although the reaction was immediate and widespread, little Minis were rather beneath Hooper, who did not pursue the idea.

Harold Radford did. He thought it was a superb plan and set-to with a will. He also had a history with Rolls-Royce, having spent time kitting them out with cocktail cabinets and the like. By 1963, he had a stand at the Motor Show on which was a Mini containing much of his craft. The company became part of H. R. Owen, the exotic car dealership, who for a few years attempted to mass-produce the craftsmanship. It worked for a while because the ballyhoo of the publicity kept the steam up. But it was not a sound basis for a coachbuilding business and it passed into the hands of John Kary and finally faded from view.

Having started the thing off, Peter Sellers made himself a customer of Radford and bought another Mini from them which had an opening tailgate. Eddie Collins, the marketing man in the Radford organization, left to join Wood and Pickett—another London coachbuilder, which made the Margrave Mini conversions. The firm was formed when two craftsmen, Bill Wood and Les Pickett, left Hoopers during a strike to work for themselves. Their first customer was Hayley Mills.

It was run on a much sounder basis. The customer specified what he wanted and spent anything from £300 to £8000 on putting living-room luxury into a Mini. Collins and Sellers met up again when the actor ordered a Margrave Mini for the lovely Britt Ekland.

There have been other names in the game and there are literally hundreds of small companies adding their own versions of how the Mini can be improved, but perhaps the best of the rest were the Bertone-styled Cooper VIP and the Oyler. When the Cooper Car Company saw how

The early ideas about
distinction involved giving the
Mini mock wickerwork side
panels

Ernest Marples's Cooper S
with a rear door was created at
Longbridge by Dick Gallimore

Opposite, above It is hard to
imagine a busier facia in a
Mini. This was a Radford
conversion

Opposite A light idea from an
ingenious owner. Wood and
Pickett supplied the skill when
the owner asked to travel
behind a pool of Mercedes-
Benz illumination. Not the
Omar you are thinking of—this
one preferred to stay
anonymous

effectively the coachbuilders were increasing the value of Mini Coopers,
it decided to take the plunge. Its answer was to commission the Italian
styling house Bertone to redesign the interior. The result was very
attractive but never went into production. Oyler, on the other hand, was a
seating company which moved into Mini improving in the mid-seventies
and offered two levels of trim. Their products were called Contessa and
Gloria. So successful were they that in 1976 *Motor* magazine was
persuaded to list Oyler as a motor manufacturer.

The first Radford Mini of pre-Motor Show 1963 was known as the
Cooper Mini de Ville Grande Luxe. The car that carried the Radford
demonstrator number plate (R 1000) that year, had redesigned seats in
white leather. The mantlepiece was completely redesigned with an
instrument binnacle over the steering column. It was twin-tone in Rolls-
Royce charcoal and Bentley silver with electric window lifts, rear
demister, Webasto sun roof, stereo radio and lamb's-wool carpets. The
impact was devastating and the price of £1100 was dazzling to the Mini
owner of the day.

Features that were criticized and subsequently remedied were
numerous. The extra weight of all the bits and pieces slowed the car down
and Radford eventually teamed up with Downton to make sure that the
luxury car was at least as fast as the standard Cooper. An arm-rest

161

between the two fronts seats obstructed access to the handbrake, the sun shining through the roof on to the chrome spokes of the steering wheel dazzled the driver, and the rev counter was invisible to the driver placing his hands on the wheel at the recommended ten to two position. The grab handle on the door dealt the elbow a severe crack when the wheel was being spun in anger. Worse, the gear-change rattle of the standard Mini was very, very obvious.

By January 1966, R 1000 was screwed to a dark blue 1275 Cooper S priced at £1650. Fully reclining all-leather bucket seats sat on floor-covering sumptuously thick. On top of the original carpet was $\frac{3}{4}$-inch underfelt, an inch of foam and $1\frac{1}{2}$ inches of nylon pile carpet. With so

The Bertone-styled Cooper S VIP commissioned by the Cooper Car Company from the Italian styling house back here in England

Another way of giving a Mini three doors. Radford again

much sound deadening, the only way it was possible to tell the engine was running was from the rev counter flickering around 750 rpm. It was a real effort to sink the pedals to the floor, and an acquired art. The gear rattle was cured and the wind roar round the Webasto improved with a special deflector. It had Cosmic alloy road wheels, and £120 worth of Downton engine conversion clipped nearly six seconds off the Cooper's 0 to 60 mph acceleration time to bring the figure below twelve seconds. The body was completely resprayed, and trimmed with chrome. Doors were panelled in blue leather with red warning lights at the trailing edge which lit when the doors were opened and were a very advanced feature. Electric windows, underseal, safety belts, wing mirrors, interior dipping mirror, heated rear screen, burglar alarm and air horns with transfer switch completed the list of add-on bits. A Radford special feature was a two-piece folding rear seat in the same blue leather that created a platform for unwieldy pieces of luggage. The price of the basic car at that time was a mere £778, but Radford was sufficiently famous to attract three sales a week in addition to its part conversion work.

Cooper's own version of the art was slightly more workaday. A set of blueprints was despatched to Bertone in 1966 along with a standard car which came back with the Italian job completed. Externally it was unchanged except that it had a new grille, Riley Elf bumpers and sidelights and rear lamp clusters that foreshadowed the change on the production car a year later. All seats and facings were stripped and reupholstered in top-quality leathercloth. Front seats were shaped to give

163

Opposite The 'off-the-peg' Wood and Pickett specification was called the Margrave, here with nudge bars

Opposite, below Twin headlamps and stiff nudge bar signal the approach of the Margrave Mini

lateral support to driver and passenger and given head restraints that rather impeded the rearward view. Seats raked and were low, and the steering column was lowered to suit. The capacious door-pockets were removed to allow fitment of electric windows, and swivelling quarter lights operated by a knurled knob just below the window itself. The door was opened by a recessed catch level with the driver's knee, just above the switch for the electric windows. Like Radford, Bertone found no way of improving on the familiar black fascia plate for the Mini heater control. Beneath the panel that contained it was an ashtray, the control for the passenger window lift and a small but efficient radio. The two main instruments and the four common subsidiary dials for fuel, water, oil and battery charge were contained in one ribbed aluminium panel, while to the left of it was another containing five switches and three warning lights. The whole was surrounded, top and bottom, with padded crash rolls.

The arrival in Britain of Arab oil money made almost anything possible, and in the late nineteen-seventies Wood and Pickett was building Minis worth anything up to £20,000. The price was quite easy to achieve without resorting to gold leaf. Several items cost more than £500 apiece and included a complete respray inside and out with ten coats of

The ultimate luxury. The interior of the Mini Wood and Pickett built for the 1977 motor show at Earls Court

paint, air conditioning, radio telephone, colour television, quadrophonics, leather trimming, rebuilt facia, a pair of the best seats, deseaming and wheel-arch extensions, electric sun-roof, electric windows with tinted glass, fold-down rear seat conversion, five new wheels and tyres.

The price had already reached more than £10,000, including the price of the car, before you paused to think about trivia like courtesy lights, carpets, soundproofing and engine tuning.

Buttoned leather upholstery and fake hood irons mark out another multi-thousand-pound Wood and Pickett classic

12 Minispecials

The sub-frame arrangement of the Mini made it the easiest car from which to pirate the power pack. In consequence, there grew up around the Mini a vast and varied industry of specialist car-builders who each stamped their own personality on the little car. Some were just one-offs and they formed the majority, but others were so admired that the creators were flattered into taking up series-production, mostly in kit form to avoid Purchase Tax. Some have survived, others are just a memory so thin that no one can recall the shape that went with the name. A very few are still in series-production in a precarious industry that threatens to break or bankrupt even the most skilled engineers and capable accountants.

Two cars, the Marcos and the Unipower, are cherished by proud owners' clubs which commemorate, respectively, the most numerous Mini-special and the best. Of the scores of home-made one-offs, two deserve particular mention, the Boro GT and the Micron.

Two very special specials had only three wheels. One was a road-going vehicle with a rigid backbone chassis that the rider sat astride with the engine between two wheels up ahead. There was no bodywork. The other was built specifically to comply with the regulations for racing motorcycle and sidecar and was very successful.

Mini Sprint

The activity that surrounded the creation of the Mini Sprint was so rapid and so short-lived that it had many people believing that it had all been an illusion. Clive Trickey, the successful club racer and regular *Cars and Car Conversions* magazine contributor, demonstrated the idea. Geoff Thomas Distribution designed and marketed the cut-down car as a

GTS, and it was then taken over by Rob Walker (the man behind Stirling Moss), became the Walker GTS, and finally ended up as the Mini Sprint and the property of the coachbuilder Stewart and Arden.

The first production versions left the S & A London production line early in 1967. Conversion of the standard Cooper S started with the car being stripped of all components, trim and electrics. The body-shell was lowered by removing one and half inches between the floor and the waistline and a similar amount from between waist and roof. All the external welded flanges were removed and transformed into butt or lap welds, an operation known as deseaming. Standard lights were removed and the wings reshaped to accept rectangular Cibies. These emphasized the lower line, gave a new frontal appearance and improved the illumination of the road. Front seat frames were lowered and the seat reclined to cope with the lower line of sight. A second series of cars—known as Sprint GTs—took the roof down a further one and a quarter inches.

None of these three cut-down Minis appear to be the genuine article Mini Sprints but they illustrate the illusion well. Presumably the owners have had to take three inches out of the seat height too

The rake of both front and rear screen was increased, which was claimed to improve the aerodynamics. Whether it did or not, the weight decrease certainly improved performance noticeably. The first demonstrator was finished in metallic light blue with Restall seats, tiny thirteen-inch steering wheel, and 4½-inch Minilite magnesium alloy wheels. Lowering of the car made it even more stable than it was in standard form and reduced the understeer. Cost of the full conversion put the price of a Cooper S up from £850 to £1300.

An earlier version of the same thing was the Minisprint (all one word), which could be bought from the GT Equipment Company in Poole, Dorset. An exchange, cut-down body-shell cost £195, or a complete car sprayed white with an 850 cc engine was £495.

Broadspeed GT

Ralph Broad packaged his tuning wizardry in his own box in 1966–67. About twelve of his Broadspeed GTs were built for Britain with engines to the customers' specification. Sixteen more went to Spain. Like the Minisprint, it was a chop-and-change exercise over-engineered in true Broad style.

He chopped the top off a standard Mini, deseamed, lowered the suspension and reduced the overall height by five inches. The screen was raked and the rear was designed as a fastback with a bob-tail that had a slight spoiler effect. With a 1275 cc, 100 bhp engine the conversion at 1966 prices put the value of the finished car at £1500. It had limited appeal on the circuits because it was classed as a GT and had to line up with the Marcos and Diva.

Below right Fastback and bob-tail and no boot—the Broadspeed GT

Midget

Midget racing success story for the Fireball Midget of Frank Boyles

Thanks to the Mini engine and a large dose of his own ingenuity, Frank Boyles can rank himself alongside such luminaries as Colin Chapman and Bruce McLaren. In the history of motor sport, there have been few men to design, build, drive and win with their own cars. Whereas Chapman of Lotus and McLaren performed their feats in the glare of world attention, Boyles achieved the same degree of success in the relative obscurity of midget racing.

Up and down the country on the oval circuits used by stock cars, midget cars race to the Spedeworth rules—devised by journalist Tony Bostock in 1967 when he was editor of *Popular Motoring*. The wheelbase of the cars in the championship had to be no more than six feet and Boyles decided right from the start that the Mini engine, gearbox and driveshaft were the right choice for his cars. He built sixteen cars called Fireball, in four groups. The Marks I, II and IV used a 1275 cc Mini engine developing 120 bhp, while the Mark III was fitted with a Ford unit. It was not actually the power output that was all that important, and it was those who thought it was who never did any of the winning. For the oval circuits the vital attribute was low-down torque and this the Fireball had in plenty.

The drawback of using the Mini drive train—and an additional reason for optimizing torque—was that while competitors were able to change axle ratios to suit the various circuits, Fireball could not.

Apart from Fireball, there was only one series-built midget racer and that was the Geoff Rumble-designed, Ford-based Dastle. All other competitors used their own one-off machines and the only other Mini-based car that approached the Fireball success rate was the Scorpion, built and raced by Nick Bonner. For two years, 1971 and 1972, Frank Boyles won every race in which the car finished and that was most of them. With thirty-five meetings a year and three races at each meeting, that made an extraordinary total of 200 events raced and won.

Boyles retired from racing in 1975 aged thirty-three, when the commitments of two children, an expanding business and ever-increasing journey times to northern circuits began to take their toll. But he retained his Fireball racer and an unused kit Fireball which was the last to be made. The last race he took part in was a European championship event in Holland which he led but was forced to retire from when the engine overheated.

GTM

Now owned by Mike Smith, a director of KBM Autosports of Wellingborough, Northants, the GTM has a history going back to 1969. The lightweight, two-seater, closed sports car was designed by Cox and produced by Heglass-fibre engineers, Lundberg of Hartlepool. The rights to the mid-engined car were purchased by Mike Smith in 1977 and production increased to two a week. Supply was insufficient to meet demand even then. One advertisement drew 1400 inquiries.

An early GTM at an enthusiasts' meeting. This one has a non-standard vinyl roof covering

By mid-1978, seventy cars had been made under KBM control after there had been chassis and other detail changes to ease manufacture. A larger version of the ten feet eight inch car has been designed to improve luggage space. Construction is space frame and monocoque, with any of the BL A-series engines available to drive the rear wheels. A top speed of 120 mph is claimed possible with the 1275 cc engine. Prices of complete kits range from £650 to £1350 according to specification.

A Crayford Mini Convertible about to be exported to Australia as a sample in the hope that manufacture might start up there

Biota

The Biota set out to be a Mini Seven version of the Lotus Seven, but because of the height of the engine and gearbox unit, the result was never achieved. Instead of looking sleek and low, the all-enveloping Biota body was stubby, and between the years of 1969, when it first appeared at the London Racing Car Show, and 1975, when production stopped, only thirty-six were made.

Proprietor of Biota Products, John Houghton, switched the attention of the Dinnington, Sheffield, business to jobbing glass-fibre contracts. The two-seater which was designed by Houghton cost £375 in kit form initially and rose to £575 for the final package. The chassis was tubular and used the Mini sub-frames. Both 1000 cc and 1275 cc Mini engines were offered. Length was nine feet nine inches.

Crayford Convertible

The convertible Mini saloon came from Crayford in September 1963 after six months of rumours and sightings of test cars in Wales. It was inevitable that a soft top on a car so small would look like a pram and Crayford never sold a car on looks alone. But it was well built with MGB-type hood clasps, Vybak non-crack rear window, one-hand hood lowering and sufficient chassis strengthening to give eighty per cent chassis torsional surplus for racing. An inherent disadvantage was the sidescreen frame, which had to be retained for the sliding windows, although in some versions removable side windows were available.

Its official name was the Crayford Mini Sprint Convertible. Crayford would carry out the conversion for £129 in 1963.

Ogle Mini

The Ogle Mini, based on the Mini running gear, in SX 1000 form was launched in 1962 by David Ogle Limited, of Letchworth. Production of the 2+2 rose to six a week by 1963 but stopped soon after David Ogle's death in a road accident.

Ogle is an industrial design team which did one-piece glass-fibre bodies as a side-line. The first car from the company was a special-bodied Riley 1.5. Its designs were carried into the nineteen-seventies by the Reliant Scimitar.

After the launch, John Whitmore and Andrew Hedges went on a coast-to-coast promotional tour of America. No business resulted but for one

An Ogle publicity hand-out photograph for their Mini-based coupé

order—Whitmore bought a car for his wife. It did 94 mph with an MG 1100 engine, 0 to 60 mph in fourteen seconds and twenty-six miles to the gallon.

During a slack period in the boat business, Norman Fletcher of Walsall decided that some capacity could be turned over to car manufacture. He bought the Ogle designs and moulds and one of his engineers, Paul Riley, spent two months producing the first car. They admired the Ogle design and the only modification made was to remove the bob-tail of the car. It went to the Racing Car Show with the name of Fletcher GT, and with an extremely lavish interior specification of wood, leather and a thick pile carpet.

Executives of Jensen saw it there and borrowed it for appraisal for a fortnight to consider it for larger-scale production. Only four cars were ever built because there was no supply co-operation from BMC. To build the last two, Riley had to buy 1275 cc Coopers and strip them for the parts.

A car was raced with good results; as a prototype GT it was up against Lotus and Ginetta, but despite being of the smallest capacity managed a fourth place at Brands with John Handley driving. The project never made any money for Fletcher International Sports Boats and the moulds were sold in 1967 to a business in Scotland.

The original works racing Unipower photographed in 1977

Unipower

Considered the Rolls-Royce of the Mini specials, the Unipower has been out of production since January 1970. It was made by Andrew Hedges and Tim Powell under the control of Universal Power Drives, of Perivale, Middlesex, a company whose main line of business was forestry tractors. Production of the car, which stood forty-one inches high, lasted only four years and seventy-five were made. Half that number could still be traced in Britain in 1978.

To sell the Unipower as a kit car was just a dodge to get round the law. All the owner had to do after paying his money (£1200 in 1968) was to fit the engine. The Unipower was built from a tubular steel chassis with glass-fibre body laminated in a mould owned by Specialised Mouldings. Any of the Mini range of engines could be used, fitted amidships just ahead of a large luggage box. The car weighed only just over half a ton, four hundredweight lighter than the standard Cooper S, and was therefore considerably quicker. What killed Unipower was the time lavished on each example. Even at what was then considered a very high price, the return did not justify the outlay.

Mini Status is, perhaps, similar in design to that of the successful Lotus Elite currently being sold

Mini Status

If the Mini Status has the look of the Lotus Elite, there is a logical explanation. Brian Luff, the owner and designer of the car, worked at

Lotus until 1970, and John Frayling, a freelance stylist, was responsible for the Elite (and the original nineteen-fifties Elite) and gave Luff styling assistance for the Status.

The Status was code-named 365 because it was considered suitable for every day of the year. Since production started in 1969, about fifty-five bodies have been sold, but only twenty-one production numbers had been allocated by mid-1978 because many of the bodies were purchased for outlandish projects which never saw the light of day.

The car was self-coloured orange fibre-glass, a production colour the Norwich laminator was reluctant to change to avoid having to clean the mould.

The Status project was run by Luff more or less as a hobby on a cash-with-order basis from Jersey. He is a director of the design company

Takron International, which, among other things, earns royalties on the very successful Black and Decker Workmate. Luff was a founder of the Clan project. He left when it went into volume production in 1970, and picked up some of the pieces when the company collapsed. As a product, the Imp-engined Clan was one of the most successful kit cars ever made.

Minipower

Another Brian Luff special was the Minipower—a contemporary of the Unipower which owed more to the Lotus Seven for its design brief. It was an open, rear-engined car with a very sophisticated technical specification. The suspension was a crib of current Formula One rocking-lever wishbone technology, and the whole car was designed in the kitchen of Luff's Norwich home. He had to remove the window to launch the pattern to a disinterested world. Luff describes the venture as 'casting pearls before swine'.

With a weight ratio of 40:60 front to rear, and a wide track of four feet eight inches the car did reasonably well at hillclimbs. But as the car was as expensive as the Unipower, while lacking the same road-going appeal, only twenty were ever made. Luff was only earning £10 a week for himself during the period of manufacture, and the idea was dropped.

A third Mini-based Luff idea came up during 1978. It was a glass-fibre version of the Mini Sprint idea, which created a coupé from the Mini by shortening the screen pillars and fitting special glass. The Mini Minus, however, lowered the car by shortening the whole body and the ride height, and kept the car more in proportion.

Luff was known for his dislike of marketing gimmicks and many of his projects were not only money-making in their own right but also a private send-up of other commercial ventures. The first thing he made money from when he went out in business on his own was a gear-lever knob marked with the position of eight speeds. 'The Lotus at the time was being sold with a five-speed gearbox, which made the performance worse than with the standard four-speed box, but for status reasons people demanded it, so it was supplied.'

The Rolls-grilled Mini was the perfect tease. Luff reckoned that Rolls-Royce buyers were only paying for the grille, so he provided the grille with a Mini running along behind. He managed to sell about eighty examples of the glass-fibre bonnet and plastic grille for about £20 in 1971, while Rolls-Royce Motors became increasingly unhappy. Eventually, threats of legal action became so heavy that Luff stopped production well satisfied with his joke.

Scamp

When Leyland discontinued manufacture of the Moke in 1968 and produced kits at Longbridge only for overseas assembly, one man in Surrey saw an opportunity for himself. Robert Mandry, proprietor of the Connaught Garage near Brookwood, considered the formula of a small,

Brian Luff's Minipower from above. It was hoped to out-price and perform with the Lotus Seven

Glass-fibre bonnet and plastic grille in the Rolls-Royce shape was Luff's idea of a joke. He sold about 80 examples.

Scamp-Moke. This is a Mark I version, of which around 700 were sold

open car a valuable one. He set to and built his own replacement for the Moke in prototype form without the benefit of a single drawing. He then subcontracted the work of making the aluminium body sections and by 1969 had a complete kit on the market. Within ten years, he sold 700 examples.

On 14 June 1978, he called a Press conference for a few specialist motoring writers to unveil the Mark II version, in which more than £50,000 had been invested. This time, an artist had been used to sketch the design required. The last Mark I produced in February 1978 had become illegal because the headlamps were too low. The successor did far more than just remedy the fault. It disposed of the use of the rear Mini sub-frame so that the load platform could be built to almost any length supported by almost any number of bogey wheels. All the weight that Issigonis carefully moved to the rear of the Mini to create the right balance, Robert Mandry moved back to the front (petrol tank, battery, spare wheel) so that there was the maximum weight over the drive wheels and the best counterbalance for heavy loads.

Wheels were increased in size to twelve inches (as fitted on the Hillman Imp) to cope with the extra cargo capacity and shod with heavy-duty cross-country tyres. But the most sophisticated aspect was to create a hard-top with gull-wing doors which bolted over the two seats and folding screen. An extensive range of extras was also created to add to the basic price of £385 for the body and about £150 for the hard-top.

The Scamp Mark II uses less of the Mini mechanicals than did its predecessor. Here it is using Hillman Imp front wheels

Jimini

Another imitator of the Mini-Moke, this one in a tidy steel shape, was the Weybridge-built Jimini. About 150 were turned out by RJB Electronics, but financial difficulties ended the run in 1977.

It was a popular platform for the Mini engine. The roof and sidescreens offered much better noise suppression and weather protection than could be expected. Many of the Jiminis went abroad. One of the last built is pictured and was bought by Phil Belcher, of Willenhall, for an undersealed and delivered price of £440.

Mini Marcos

The Mini Marcos is the glass-fibre variation of the Mini that has the longest record of continuous production, going back to 1965.

As the name suggests, it was born to Marcos Cars of Wiltshire, which in turn got its name from Jem Marsh and Frank Costin. These two designers used aircraft design to construct a successful GT car whose chassis and lower body was marine ply. It used a Ford 105E engine and gearbox and won many GT races in 1961 and 1962.

The Mini Marcos had a glass-fibre body/chassis unit which accepted Mini mechanicals and followed the same race-winning formula. In 1966, the year after its launch, it was the only British car to finish the 24-Hour Le Mans race. When, in 1970, Marcos produced the disastrous, futuristic

179

Opposite The Jimini was more Moke-like than most of its rivals

Opposite below A very late model Mini Marcos shows little design change from the original in 1965

Mantis, the specialist sports car market was in recession and the business collapsed. The Mini Marcos wing of the operation was, however, preserved by Jem Marsh himself and by Rob Walker, then West Country garage group owner. In 1975, the present owner, D & H Fibreglass Techniques, of Heybottom Mill, Oak View Road, Greenfield, Oldham, Lancashire, bought the rights.

Proprietor Harold Dermott, who was already in the fibre-glass business, changed the production process to self-coloured fibre-glass, increased production of kits to two a week and priced them (mid-1978) at a basic £645. Mr Dermott at one time traced the historic Le Mans car to Paris, where it was being offered for sale. The following day it was stolen and since then there have been several reports of 'sightings', but the version offered has never been the authentic one.

Landar

Probably the fastest racing special ever built around Mini Cooper mechanicals was the Birmingham Landar. It was built like a miniature Can-Am car, stood only thirty inches high and had such low drag that at Oulton Park it was clocked at 140 mph.

The Landar was perhaps the fastest, and certainly the most successful, of the Mini-based racing cars

The designers and builders of the car were the Radnall Brothers (the car's name reversed), who run the cycle component manufacturer A. E. Radnall, Birmingham. There were two phases; the R6 had a space frame with glass-fibre bodywork and a rear end that was entirely Mini sub-frame. The two-seater open bodywork by Williams and Prichard made

it an out-and-out racing car, and without an engine it cost £900 in 1965. Production started in 1963 and about forty were built.

The R7 was rather more sophisticated and was built completely around a space frame with the engine still transverse and mounted at the back but canted twenty degrees forward. It was built to comply with the Firestone F100 Formula for 1300s and was given its competition debut by Tony Lanfranchi.

Quite a few of the cars were exported to America, which became the biggest single market, and the greatest competitive success was winning the Sports Car Club of America under 1300 cc sports car championship.

Fewer than ten of the R7s were built. The operation was a loss-maker as so often happened, and in 1970, when the Radnall business moved out of Birmingham, building ceased.

In 1972, the moulds were sold to a Canadian, who intended small-scale production in Nova Scotia.

Mini Se7en Club

The Mini Se7en Club—still going strong in four national centres—was founded by a group of enthusiasts in 1961 in London. With Mini ownership, it grew. When it reached the point where a team of six or seven enthusiasts were trying to distribute 700 magazines every month, the time had come to inaugurate local centres. By the end of 1962 there were six, at Birmingham, Bristol, Brighouse, Luton, Nottingham and Lincoln. There were nine regions where an active centre operated but only ever seven at one time. Strong centres also emerged in Holland, Belgium, New Zealand, Australia, Sweden and Czechoslovakia.

The club started the *Mini Mag*, which was without doubt the most professional non-professional car magazine in the business. Despite the competition activity that surrounded the Mini, it was not until 1965 that the club felt strong enough to organize its own race meeting. On 13 June at Snetterton it ran the first Whitmore Trophy Race—named after the famous Sir John, who was a consistent Mini winner until the young John Fitzpatrick hove into view. The race meeting was organized by Maurice Burton and it made money—the only one of fifty-seven successive meetings to do so.

Trouble was brewing because the racing side was not accountable separately from the M7C and it was running at the expense of non-racing members. Burton started a register and the racing members transferred to the M7C Racing Centre. It had a successful race-organizing team which was invited to launch the very first All-Saloon Car Race Meeting at Brands Hatch on 13 February 1966.

In September of 1967 there was a move towards abandoning national control of the club in favour of making local centres autonomous. BMC began to sniff around and decided on 8 January 1968 that Maurice Burton should be sponsored in his secretarial duties and he was given an office at Abingdon. BMC's interest had been stirred by the fact that the British Saloon Racing Club had tried to take the M7C over as an expansionist move and at the Racing Car Show that year there had been a Hillman Imp on the M7C stand.

That had been too much for the then BMC publicity director who became front-man of the television programme *Tomorrow's World*, Raymond Baxter.

There were nearly 1000 members at that stage under the chairmanship of John Stanton.

Baxter became a director of the club, which boasted as President and vice-President respectively John Cooper and Graham Hill.

In 1969, there was a feeling that the rather vague factory control of the club—following the merger with Leyland—should be ended.

The move was led by Dave Orchard, secretary of the Midland centre, who successfully lobbied the executive.

But any action the club could take was pre-empted by the company. The first Orchard knew of the success of his campaign was an advert in November 1969 in *The Birmingham Post*, which announced British Motor Holdings—as it then was—had severed all connections with the M7C.

Race meetings began to fade out even though there was an RAC-approved Mini 7 Formula.

The 750 Motor Club continued races for Minis and mounted the second take-over for the racing centre.

Stanton warned of the bid and decided that the only way that the shambles of the racing centre could be sorted out was to raise £500.

The deficit had accrued because each meeting organized by the racing centre had been paid for by the entry fees for the next one.

When racing stopped there was bound to be a shortage.

Four people decided that the M7C Racing Centre name must be preserved and donated £100 each to the fund. The other £100 came more slowly.

A new chairman took over—a man whose main interest was amateur dramatics, Peter Haskins.

He had become interested in the club because his next-door neighbour was a member. He wanted to find out what made the club tick and found that the answer at that time was very little.

The *Mini Mag* died in 1969 after a succession of editors failed to arouse any enthusiasm among contributors.

In 1971, Leyland suddenly realized how much was lost by not having an active owner's club and approached the M7C to mastermind the Mini racing championship.

Mini racers remained members of the M7C Racing Centre, which thrived again. The parent club—with no magazine—was reduced in status to association, while three regional centres now organize social events for the faithful. Dave Orchard of Bromsgrove is association secretary and dedicated to the Mini history. His house groans under the weight of all the accumulated records.

Motley Mini grid at a Brands Hatch Festival. A front row of lowered Minis with oblong lights showing the change of outline when the seams (left) are removed (right).

A union jack roof, multi-coloured Cooper and Crayford Convertible on the second row are followed by a Marcos and a Unipower. The covered wagon at the back is a Moke with all-enclosing hard-top, probably the work of the Barton Motor Company of Plymouth, who turned a Moke into a roomy estate car for £133 in mid-1966

185

The ingenious Mini Se7en Club published in May 1962 some new definitions for established words.

Jasmin: Chris Barber's
Ermine: the second car
Miniscule: driving school for dwarfs
Ominous: trolleybus replacement
Minestrone: souped up
Ministry: for those with dogs
Determine: a move to ban Minis from saloon races
Examine: eight-sided Mini

Opposite and overleaf (all) The 20th anniversary of the Mini could not be allowed to pass without a party.
On a blisteringly hot summer's weekend in 1979, disc jockey Noel Edmunds and anybody who was anybody in the Mini world headed for Donington race circuit in Leicestershire.
Topped and chopped – the shortest short cut yet drew astonishment at 25th party.

The 25th Anniversary party at Donington brought out yards of Minis

Below There's only one way to give a Mini a lift and that is on the back of a long wheelbase Mini pick-up. Mike Chaplin made sure that his customized saloon made it to the Donington Mini extravaganza by ferrying it there in style

13 Mini Special Edition

Once the separation of Mini and Metro had occurred, the marketing department took over the fortunes of the little car. It was for the salesmen rather than the engineers to suspend the ageing process by presenting Mini well rather than resorting to physical change; cosmetics not facelifts.

The engineers were always there to fall back on. If legislation were to outlaw the car for some detail that fell foul of modern safety requirements, then flange covers and radiator surrounds, flush door handles and fascia changes were all ready.

But the threat of legislative change remained just a threat, and the engineers merely contributed hardened valve seats for unleaded fuel, catalysts for European and Japanese markets and such ephemeral legislative details as headlights adjustable from the cabin – required by the Germans.

Japan had become rather important. The increasingly wealthy and novelty-hungry Japanese rediscoverd the Mini in 1985 and within three years sales had quadrupled. (This book was translated into Japanese and published there in 1986 – helping the love affair.)

John Cooper got involved too – providing crated kits that allowed enthusiasts to convert the new Mini into a Sixties Cooper replica.

Had the same specification been attempted by the manufacturer, there would have been a requirement to resubmit Mini for Type Approval which would not have been forthcoming. That is why there will never be a Mini with a high-performance MG Metro engine for example, even though such a thing is technically possible.

At Canley in Coventry, Rover Group stylists under Gordon Sked and Martin Peach lead the task of dreaming up the limited editions which started with a trickle but which by 1989 had become a flood of five within as many months.

They were not always popular with the manufacturers at Longbridge when their ideas were presented.

The Ritz was the first Mayfair-derived limited edition in 1985

Multi-fabric upholstery? No thanks. Colour-co-ordinated roof? You must be joking. Pearlesquent paint? That needs new plant.

But gradually the difficulties were overcome. New concepts began to fall into a pattern, with internal to external colour co-ordination being key and increasingly bold use of colour being taken through to seat belts, steering wheels, flashing, badging and detailing.

Success arose from the established fact that Mini was able to transcend class. The people who were not buying the City because of its price were buying the Mayfair and the limited edition models because they made acceptable statements about life-style. Many people like a car to say something about their taste; few are confident enough to compose that statement themselves. Bespoke individuality is the perfect compromise.

As the new ways of presenting Mini were being compiled, the car found itself with a new champion. Sir Graham Day, the chairman of Rover brought in from British Shipbuilders who negotiated the sale of Rover to British Aerospace in 1988, found that demand for Mini exceeded the commitment to build it. One of his first public statements after reviewing the company was that the marketing impetus would resume.

With campaigns such as: *Minis Have Feelings Too* given wide exposure, the car continued to fulfill its potential and to generate profit.

The 20th Anniversary specials – the Silver and the Rose – had been the first toe in the water for limited editions in 1979. Their success marked the departure from HLs and HLEs and other cryptic nomenclature and the separation into City and Mayfair.

By 1984 it was time for Mini 25 – in silver of course – for the 25th Anniversary. The following year the launch party was for the Ritz – a derivative of the Mayfair with velvet seats and alloy wheels.

For a while, the policy of grandiose names was followed slavishly with Chelsea and Piccadilly in 1986, and Park Lane the following year. The Chelsea was the first real 'designer' car with complementary interior and exterior graphics. Piccadilly was a re-run of the Ritz but with a different colour theme. The feed-back from dealers was that it was under-stated – too discreet.

Park Lane in 1987
demonstrated the first strong
graphic treatment

In the Park Lane therefore, the graphics treatment was very strong with black the dominant colour. Mini owners have always liked selecting colour from Henry Ford's original palette, and there is a higher proportion of Minis in black than any other car.

There was to have been a Mini called Wimbledon but after much of the graphics preparation had been done the authorities of that august club felt unable to share. The design think tank had to volly quickly and spun in the Advantage which became a familiar sight during promotions at the tennis championships of 1987.

The Wimbledon classic in 1987
turned a naming problem to
Advantage

Colour commitments were getting stronger. Jet Black and Red Hot were cued in 1988 with particular trouble taken in finding just the right red. There had been a trace of embarrassment about the Rover red. It was far from vivid because the company had a commitment to lead-free paint and without lead, the pigmentation was never a great success. So the designers eventually adopted the Post Office's pillar-box red even though they knew from painting PO vans that it required special and rather difficult application.

Once design started to take on such great importance there was a temptation to bring in the big-name designers. Mary Quant – the mini-skirt pioneer of the Swinging Sixties was an obvious choice. Her ideas for grey replacing chrome, daisy logos and zebra-striped seats were fairly faithfully followed, but the Quant name was supplanted by Designer when pre-launch product clinics discovered that Joe Public did not want Mary's name on the side of his car.

A very small Quant signature did, however, remain on the bonnet badge.

The Designer label rekindled the Quant association in 1988

Jet Black and Red Hot in 1988. Black was the better seller.

Then came the abundance of 1989 and a flush of four cars in February which relied for their image entirely on colour with just a faint echo of the magnificent Mini Cooper and its distinctive white roof and Minilite wheels.

Rose and Sky took the pastel theme colours through the badging and upholstery to the roof, while the Racing (green) and Flame (red) had the no-nonsense pure white roof of the Sixties hard-charger.

The honey of the bunch for 1989 of course was the Mini 30. Launched in June in time for the August 28th anniversary party at Silverstone, the Mini 30 was to be the first Rover product with pearlescent paint. The technology was just becoming available at Longbridge in preparation for the company's forthcoming new mid-range car. By a happy chance, pearl is the designated token for 30th anniveraries.

The car had the most attractive specification ever to emerge from the factory with proper cast Minilite-replica alloy wheels, leather seat facings, painted wheel-arch spats, electronic radio cassette, hockey-stick gear-lever and new gaiter. The striking deep-lustre red was expected to take most of the proposed 3,000 sales in the UK, but demand from abroad for black was so strong that a black option was also prepared by the Mini marketing strategy manager, Rod Kirkpatrick.

Any of the Sixties coach-builders would have been proud of the result but none would have managed what the factory achieved – a price premium of less than 10 per cent on the basic car.

Appendices

Model development

Mini 850

1959	*August*	Basic and de-luxe saloons introduced. (Austin Seven and Morris Mini Minor, ADO 15.)
1960	*April*	Driveshaft splines changed from square section to involute from: Austin AA2S7 26590, Morris MA2S4 24831.
	September/ October	Countryman/Traveller Estate cars introduced with 'wood-framed' body.
1961	*May*	Alternative cast aluminium suspension trumpets introduced from: Austin AA2S7 123291, Morris MA2S4 70376.
	September	Super saloon introduced (oil pressure gauge and water temperature gauge in oval panel, key-start ignition switch in lieu of floor-mounted starter button, Duotone paint scheme and minor trim changes).
1962	*January*	Austin model now known as Austin Mini, not Seven.
	October	De-luxe and Super models replaced by single Super de-luxe model. Progressive introduction of gearboxes with baulk ring, synchromesh on upper three ratios. Option of Estate car without wood framing at lower price.
1964	*February*	Wiper arc reduced from 130° to 120° to avoid fouling screen rubber.

Wavy grille and shield badge denote Austin Seven, to be renamed Austin Mini

The second type of gear-change following the 'straight stick', with the bootlace door release and twin auxiliary instruments

The first Mini with de-luxe interior

The first estate without the wood

	September	Improved gearboxes (commonization with Cooper, etc.) with 'B' series tooth sizes, needle roller bearings (progressive introduction, then 100% fit from Austin engine 8AM UH 803601 and equivalent Morris number). New change speed forks with increased contact area (from Austin engine 8AM UH 795957). Diaphragm spring clutch introduced. Hydrolastic suspension introduced on saloons only. Twin leading shoe front brakes introduced. Minor trim changes.
	November	3-position seat brackets fitted to driver's seat.
1965	*January/ May October*	'Scroll'-type oil seal on primary gear. Automatic gearbox option introduced with corresponding uprated engine (HS 4 carburetter, etc). NB: 850 automatic only supplied for special contracts now.
1966	*January*	Safety 'bosses' fitted under leading edge of door handles. Smoother action clutch fitted.
1967	*October*	Mk II models introduced—standard and Super de-luxe saloons with wider rear window, new larger front grille, new badging and interior trim, improved seats, etc.

The new rear lights and wider rear window on the Mark II of 1967

	October/ November	Moulded plastic cooling fan fitted.
1968	*June/July*	Cable-type internal door release replaced by handle.
	September	All synchromesh gearbox introduced (signified by engine number reverting to 101).
	October	Mk II models replaced by ADO 20 series saloon 850 with wind-up windows, concealed door hinges and dry cone suspension. Negative earth electrics—mechanical fuel pump.
1969	*April/May*	Heated rear window option introduced, from saloon 215S 097882A.
1970	*October/ November*	Ignition shield fitted from D20S 017238L.
1972	*February/ March*	Improved synchromesh from engine 85H 387E H 109003.
	April/May	Split type needle roller bearings fitted to idler gears—progressive introduction up to engine 85H 387E H 125102 then 100% fit.
1972/ 73	*December/ January*	Improved drive shaft boot, longer life from chassis 799557A. Alternator becomes standard fit. Rod shift gear-change introduced from Commission D20S 59998A.
1973	*April/May*	New driveshaft with plunging CV inboard joints, introduced from Commission D20S 70304A (offset sphere, bi-podal type).
	June/July	Improved door check pivot brackets introduced.
	October	Low octane fuel distribution for Mini 850 saloon discontinued.
1974	*February*	Inertia reel seat belts fitted as standard.
	April	Heater standard on Mini 850.
	May	H54 carburetter, revised manifold, air cleaner and exhaust manifold fitted. Ignition timing altered static 6° BTDC stroboscopic 11° BTDC (ECE15 33 bhp DIN).
	July	Passenger sun visor fitted as standard.
1975	*October*	88° Thermostat fitted as standard. New seat frames and trim with anti-tip catches.
1976	*May*	Twin stalk controls, heated rear window, radial tyres, hazard lights, new sub-frame mounts, new ignition lock, larger pedals.
1977	*August*	Matt black grille, revised steering wheel.
1979	*July*	Mini City with black bumpers and wheelarches.
	August	Discontinued

Mini 1000

1967	*October*	1000 Super de-luxe saloon and estate (with or without wood trim) introduced. With 998 cc

Super de-luxe Mini 1000 Mk II for 1967. Badging persists and this one is a Morris, but rationalization has struck and the Morris wheel-trim with oblong cut-out shapes has been replaced by Austin's half-moons

The Mini 1000 was distinguished by a matt black grille in August of 1977 while inside the standard trim was striped nylon upholstery

engine, Mk II body, remote Cooper-type gearshift and optional automatic gearbox.

	October/ November	Moulded plastic cooling fan fitted.
1968	*June/July*	Cable-type internal door release replaced by handle.
	August	All synchromesh gearbox introduced.
1969	*April/May*	Heated rear window, option introduced.
	October	Mk II Super de-luxe replaced by Mini 1000 with wind-up windows, concealed door hinges, dry cone suspension, negative earth electrics, opening rear quarterlights, etc. Mechanical fuel pump. Mk II estate car discontinued (replaced by Clubman Estate).
1970	*October/ November*	Ignition shield fitted from commission N20S 005411L/N20S 47756A.
1972	*February/ March*	Improved synchromesh from engine 99H 353EH 275337.
	April/May	Split-type needle roller bearings fitted to idler gears, progressive introduction up to engine 99H 353EH 309615 then 100% fit.

Two giant's-eye views of first, the Mini 1000 (1968 model) and an early Clubman

The 1976 Clubman facia

A very early Clubman salo

SOK 878H

1972/	December/	Improved drive shaft boot, longer life, from
73	January	chassis 799401A. Alternator becomes standard fit from commission N20S 165797A. Rod shift gear-change introduced from commission N20S 178371A.
	April/May	New drive shaft introduced with plunging CV inboard joints (offset sphere, bi-podal type).
	June/July	Improved door check pivot bracket fitted.
1974	January	Automatic gearbox now only available as option on home sales.
	February	Inertia reel seat belts fitted as standard.
	May	H54 carburetter, revised manifold, air cleaner and exhaust manifold fitted, revised ignition timing static 4° BTDC stroboscopic 7° BTDC at 1000 rpm (ECE 15 Tune 39 bhp DIN).
1975	October	Mini 1000 special (Limited edition) released with the following items as standard: 1) Orange-striped cloth seat trim. 2) Reclining front seats. 3) Safari carpets. 4) Two chromed door mirrors. 5) Coach-line along waist. 6) Brooklands green and glacier white body colour. 80° thermostat fitted as standard to all models.

Vinyl-coated steel takes the place of timber

Grille change for the Clubman in 1976

1976	*May*	Twin stalk controls, heated rear window, radial tyres, hazard lights, new sub-frame mounts, face-level vents, matt black grille, moulded carpets.
1977	*August*	Reclining seats, reversing lights, dipping rear-view mirror.
1979	*August*	1100S LE. Metallic silver or rose, vinyl roof and shaded band stripes. 1275GT instruments and console.
	October	Re-designated as Super, with ¾ length coachline.
1980	*September*	1000 City introduced (as 850 City).
	October	Super re-designated HL. Badging as City. 'H' pattern steering wheel, twin dials, tinted glass. Estate option available, both in manual and automatic forms.
1982	*February*	Estate discontinued.
	April	City re-designated E.
		HL re-designated HLE.
	October	HLE re-designated Mayfair.
1983	*October*	Mini Sprite LE introduced.
1984	*June*	25th Anniversary LE introduced.
	June	Front disc brakes (c/o 1275 GT).
		Modified rear brake drums (c/o 1275 GT).
		Final drive changes (3.105:1).
		12″ wheels and trim ⎫ (c/o 1275 GT).
		145/70 SR12 tyres ⎭
		New alloy wheel option.
		Wheelarch spats.
1985	*February*	The 'Chelsea' LE introduced.
	June	Mini 'Ritz' LE introduced.
	October	1986 MY introduced on City E and Mayfair: Revised interior colour keying.
		Metro style gearknob, handbrake grip (Mayfair) and steering wheels.

An 'X-ray' of Mini shows where the hush-kit went to quieten the car for the 1980s.

Opposite The Cooper S facia was nearly as spartan as the standard Mini—not even a rev counter was fitted

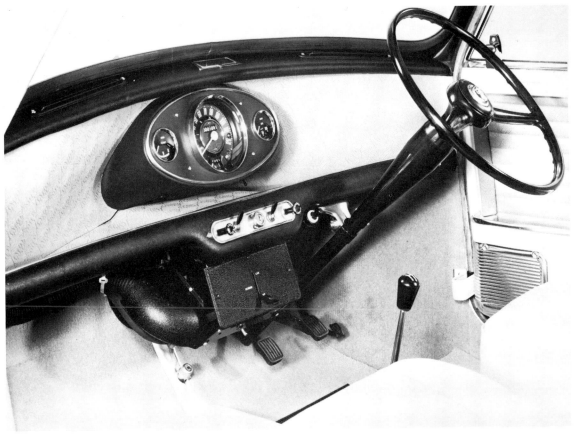

Left and below The 20-year milestone Mini. The silver grey or rose metallic Minis were introduced in 1979 on the 20th anniversary of the car. Only 2500 were proposed for the limited edition but that was quickly doubled to 5000 when the popularity became clear. The 1100 cc Special had wheel arches and a host of distinguishing internal features for a price of £3300

		Two pack instruments on City E.
		Three pack instruments on Mayfair.
		Revised steering column stalks.
		Revised seating (Mayfair).
		Grey exterior hardware.
		New wheel trims.
1986	*June*	Mini 'Piccadilly' LE introduced.
1987	*February*	Mini 'Park Lane' LE introduced.
	May	Mini 'Advantage' LE introduced.
1988	*February*	Mini 'Red Hot and Jet Black' LE introduced.
	June	Mini 'Designer' LE introduced.
	October	Mini 1989 MY introduced on City and Mayfair:

Revised interior trims, City—Crayons, Mayfair—Prism

Revised instrument graphics.

Rear seat belts.

Passenger and driver's vanity mirror.

Three-spoke steering wheel—City.

Radio/cassette player—Mayfair.

Headrests standard on City.

Revised badging.

New wheel trim on Mayfair.

Brake servo-standard fit on City and Mayfair.

Below The Sprite name was rewritten into the history books on 17 October 1983 when a limited edition of 2500 Mini Sprites was created to fill the gap between the City and the Mayfair. It had a one-litre engine, wide alloy wheels and arch extensions

Left and below The arrival of Mini 25 on July 2 1984 marked the Mini's adoption of 12 in. wheels and disc brakes all round. The cost of making 10 inch wheels and drum brakes for the Mini alone had become disproportionately expensive.

Priced on launch at £3864, Mini 25 was the most lavishly equipped Mini ever. Only 5000 were built with 1500 for export.

It had a grey/red stripe on silver bodywork, and wheelarches bumpers, grille, door handles and mirrors all picked out in nimbus.

Inside there was plush grey and red carpets and cladding, a leather steering wheel, tachometer and stereo, and a novel zipped pocket on the front of the seat squab.

In addition to the Mini Mayfair spec. there was tinted glass, reversing and fog lamps, twin exterior mirrors, face-vents and opening rear windows

The first 1275GT

Low-profile tyre technology allowed twelve-inch wheels by 1974 and bigger discs for the brakes

Mini Clubman

1969	*October*	Saloon introduced with restyled front, improved trim, seats and instrumentation, etc. Hydrolastic suspension, 998 cc engine. Clubman Estate, 998 cc engine, dry cone suspension introduced, replacing 1000 Countryman/Traveller.
1970	*October/ November*	Ignition shield introduced from: Saloon S20S 26595A, Estate 20W 8016A.
1971	*June*	Dry cone suspension introduced. Improved CV driveshaft boot for longer life from Saloon S20S 74328A, Estate 20W 49893A.
1972	*February/ March*	Improved synchromesh from engine 99H 353 EH 275337.
	April/May	Split-type needle roller bearings fitted to idler gears from engine 99H 353 EH 309615.
1972/ 73	*December/ January*	Alternator standard fit, from Saloon S20S 74727A, Estate 20W 50307A.
1973	*April/May*	Rod shift gear-change introduced, from Saloon S20S 78404A, Estate 20W 54401A.

Wood veneer mantelpiece for the Riley Elf

Postscript: Minier than Mini.
This cut and shut Mini was
photographed in Geneva by
Mini Se7en Club member,
Stuart Wyre of Birmingham

	June/July	Plunging CV joints (offset-sphere bi-podal type) on inboard end of new driveshafts, from Saloon S20S 89295A, Estate 20W 64533A. Improved door check bracket fitted.
1974	*January*	Automatic gearbox fitted as option on home sale only.
	February	Inertia reel seat belts fitted as standard.
1975	*October*	New design reclining front seats fitted as standard with anti-tilt locks. 998 cc engine replaced by 1098 cc engine as standard. If automatic gearbox is specified 998 cc engine is used.
	October	88° Thermostat fitted as standard.
1976	*May*	Twin stalk controls, heated rear window, radial tyres, hazard lights, new sub-frame mounts, ignition lock, larger pedals, moulded carpets, revised grille, new badges.
1977	*August*	Leather steering wheel, lockable filler cap, tinted glass, reversing lights.
1980	*August*	Discontinued.

Mini Cooper

1961	*October*	Saloon introduced with super trim and twin carb 997 cc engine, and disc brakes.
1963	*March*	Improved disc brakes fitted.
1964	*February*	Wiper arc reduced from 130° to 120° to avoid fouling screen rubber.

	January	997 cc engine replaced by twin carb 998 cc engine.
	March	SP41 radial tyres became standard fit.
	July	Lower pressure setting on rear brake anti-lock valve.
	September	Hydrolastic suspension introduced and slight trim changes. New change speed forks with increased contact-area, from engine 9FD SA H 1701. Diaphragm spring clutch introduced, from engine 9FA SA H 3780.
	October	New driveshaft coupling with larger bounding area for rubber to give improved torque capacity.
	November	3-position brackets fitted to driver's seat.
1965	January	13 gills per inch radiator replaced by 16 gills per inch type. (From Austin Mini Cooper commission 549774.)
	May	'Scroll'-type oil seal introduced on primary gear (from Austin Mini Cooper engines 9FD SA H 6448 and 9FD SA L 935).
	November/ December	Reclining seat option introduced.
1966	January	Safety boss fitted under leading edge of exterior door handle.
1967	October	Mk II saloons replace Mk I — Mk II bodyshell (as 850 and 1000), trim as Super de-luxe. Plastic fan fitted.
1968	September	All synchromesh gearbox introduced.
1969	April/May	Heated rear window option introduced.
	November	Mk II saloon discontinued (replaced by 1275GT).

Mini Cooper S

1963	March	S saloon introduced, based on Mini Cooper body with 1071 cc engine, larger, servo-assisted disc brakes, ventilated wheels, etc.
1964	March	1275 cc engine and 970 cc engine introduced. SP41 radial tyres standard fit.
	July	Lower pressure setting on rear brake anti-lock valve.
	August	1071 cc engine discontinued.
	September	Hydrolastic suspension introduced, also slight trim changes. Diaphragm spring clutch introduced from Austin engines 970 cc 9F SA X 29001, 1071 cc 9F SA H 33260, 1275 cc 9F SA Y 31001. Positive crankcase ventilation introduced from Austin engines 970 cc 9FD SA X 29004, 1071 cc 9FD SA H 33261, 1275 cc 9FD SA Y 31406.
	November	3-position seat brackets, fitted to driver's seat.

1965	*January*	970 cc engine discontinued.
	November/	Reclining seat option introduced.
	December	
1966	*January*	Twin petrol tanks and oil cooler made standard.
	April/May	Higher rate hydrolastic units fitted. New Steel/rubber lower wishbone bush. Taper roller rear hub bearings. Flange fixing solid universal on inboard end of driveshaft. Strengthening added to suspension mountings. From Austin C/A 257 851199, Morris K/A 254 851028.
1967	*October*	Mk II model replaces Mk I (bodyshell changes as 850/1000 Cooper). All synchromesh gearbox standard (not 100% fit until October 1968).
1969	*April/March*	Heated rear window option introduced.
1970	*March*	Mk II replaced by Mk III (ADO 20) with wind-up windows, concealed door hinges, 'Clubman'-type door trims and seats, retaining hydrolastic suspension.
	October/	Ignition shield fitted from N20 D 528A.
	November	
1971	*July*	Mk III model discontinued.

Mini 1275GT

1969	*October*	Saloon introduced with Clubman-type shell, 1275 cc single carburetter (1300) engine, servo-assisted 'S'-type disc brakes, tachometer, hydrolastic suspension, rostyle wheels, etc.
1970	*October/*	Ignition shield fitted from S20D 4147A.
	November	
1970/71	*December/ January*	Final drive ratio changed from 3.65:1 to 3.44:1 at engine 12H 389 SH 6901.
1971	*June*	Dry cone suspension introduced.
1972	*February/ March*	Improved synchromesh from engine 12H 353 EH 22958.
	April/May	Split-type needle roller bearings fitted to idler gears progressive introduction up to engine 12H 289N 20022 then 100% fit.
1972/73	*December/ January*	Improved drive shaft CV boot for longer life from car S20D 13690A. Alternator standard fit from S20D 14819A.
1973	*April/May*	Rod-shift gear-change introduced from car S20D 14922A.
	June/July	Plunging CV joints (offset-sphere bi-podal type) on inboard end of new driveshafts, from car S2 D 17134A. Improved door check bracket fitted.
1974	*February*	Inertia reel seat belts fitted as standard.
	May	Air intake system using an air temp control device introduced. (54 bhp (DIN) ECE 15 tune.)

	June	Laminated windscreen fitted as option.
	August	Denovo safety tyres fitted as option.
1975	October	(New design) reclining seats standard fitting. 88° thermostat fitted as standard.
1976	May	Twin stalk controls, revised grille, new badge, heated rear window, hazard lights, new sub-frame mounts, extra sound-deadening, moulded carpets.
1977	August	Denovo tyres standard, tinted glass, reversing lamps, locking filler cap.
1979	October	Black door mirrors and drip rail.
1980	August	Discontinued.

Riley Elf and Wolseley Hornet

1961	October	Saloons introduced with traditional 'radiator' grilles, lengthened boots, wood veneer facias, duo-tone colour schemes, etc.
1962	Autumn	Progressive introduction of baulk ring synchromesh gearboxes, leather-trimmed wearing surfaces added to seats.
	November	Mk II saloons replace Mk I, with 998 cc single-carb engine and twin leading shoe front brakes.
1964	September	Hydrolastic suspension introduced, also diaphragm spring clutch and trim changes.
1966	October	Mk III saloons replace Mk II, with wind-up windows, concealed door hinges, push-button door handles, fresh-air facia vents, Cooper-type remote control gear-changes.
1967	October/ November	Restyled seats, multi-purpose stalk switch on steering column, plastic cooling fan. Automatic gearbox option introduced.
1968	August	All synchromesh gearbox introduced.
1969	August	Mk III saloon discontinued.

Mini Van, Pick-up and Moke (LCVs)

1960	January	Van introduced, with 848 cc engine.
1961	January	Pick-up introduced, with 848 cc engine.
1962	October	Baulk ring synchromesh gearbox progressively introduced. Windscreen washers, interior light and overriders made standard fit.
1964	August	Moke introduced, utility-type body, fabric tilt roof 848 cc engine.
1967	October	998 cc engine option introduced on Van and Pick-up.
1968	October	Moke discontinued.

1969	October	Mini badges instead of marque badges, negative earth electrics, mechanical fuel pump.
1970	October/ November	Ignition shield on Van and Pick-up.
1972	February/ March	Improved synchromesh.
	April/May	Split needle roller bearings on idler gears.
1972/ 73	December/ May	Improved drive shaft boots. Alternator, standard fit. Rod shift gear-change introduced on Van and Pick-up.
1973	June/July	New driveshaft with plunging inboard CV joints.

(Main points only—many changes, as on cars)

1974	February	Automatic inertia reel seat belts fitted as standard on Pick-up.
1975	October	88°C thermostat fitted as standard.
1976	May	Twin stalk controls, inertia belts (Van), heated rear window, radial tyres, new ignition lock, larger pedals.
1978	December	Mini badge 95 indicating gross weight fitted to both van and pick-up.
1979	November	'L' pack introduced standard 998 van optional 848 van not available on pick-up. This improved level of interior trim includes cloth facing seats, carpet, passenger sun visor and extra sound insulation.
1980	November	848 pick-up discontinued.
1982	December	All derivatives of van and pick-up production ceased.

Engine data

Mini 850 (with Mk I Elf and Hornet) all models

Type	8MB
Number of cylinders	4
Bore	2.478 in. (62.94 mm)
Stroke	2.687 in. (68.26 mm)
Capacity	51.7 in³ (848 cc)
Firing order	1, 3, 4, 2
Compression ratio	8.3:1
Valve operation	Overhead by push-rod
Bmep	128 lb/in² (9 kg/cm²) at 2,900 rev/min
Torque	44 lb ft (6.08 kg m) at 2,900 rev/min

Mini 850 Automatic (see above)

Type	8AH
Compression ratio	9:1
Torque	44 lb ft (6.08 kg m) at 2,500 rev/min

Mini 1000 (with Mk II and Mk III Elf and Hornet) all models (not Cooper, City, Mayfair and City E)

Type	9WR, 99H
Bore	2.543 in. (64.588 mm)
Stroke	3.00 in. (76.2 mm)
Capacity	60.96 in³ (998 cc)
Compression ratio	8.3:1
Bmep	130 lb/in² (9.14 kg/cm²) at 2,700 rev/min
Torque	52 lb ft (7.28 kg m) at 2,700 rev/min

Mini Cooper 997

Type	9F
Bore	2.458 in. (62.43 mm)
Stroke	3.20 in. (81.28 mm)
Capacity	60.87 in³ (997 cc)
Compression ratio:	
High compression	9:1
Low compression	8.3:1
Bmep: High compression	134 lb/in² (9.42 kg/cm²) at 3,500 rev/min
Low compression	129 lb/in² (9.07 kg/cm²) at 3,500 rev /min
Torque: High compression	54 lb ft (7.46 kg m) at 3,600 rev/min
Low compression	53 lb ft (7.32 kg m) at 3,500 rev/min

Mini City, Mayfair and City E

Type	A+
Bore	2.543 in. (64.588 mm)
Stroke	3.00 in. (76.20 mm)
Capacity	60.96 in³ (998 cc)
Compression ratio	9.6:1
	8.3:1 (Rest of world only option)
Torque	50 lb ft (6.90 kg m) at 2,500 rev/min

Mini Cooper 998

Type	9FA
Bore	2.543 in. (64.588 mm)
Stroke	3.00 in. (76.2 mm)
Capacity	60.96 in³ (998 cc)
Compression ratio:	
High	9:1
Low	7.8:1
Bmep: High compression	142 lb/in² (10 kg/cm²) at 3,000 rev/min
Low compression	135 lb/in² (9.5 kg/cm²) at 3,000 rev/min
Torque: High compression	57 lb ft (7.88 kg m) at 3,000 rev/min
Low compression	56 lb ft (7.74 kg m) at 2,900 rev/min

Mini Cooper S all models

Type	970 = 9F
	1071 = 10F
	1275 = 12F

Bore (all models)	2.780 in. (70.6 mm)
Stroke: 970 cc	2.4375 in. (61.91 mm)
1071 cc	2.687 in. (68.26 mm)
1275 cc	3.2 in. (81.33 mm)
Capacity: 970 cc	59.1 in^3 (970 cc)
1071 cc	63.35 in^3 (1071 cc)
1275 cc	77.9 in^3 (1275 cc)
Compression ratio: 970 cc	10:1
1071 cc	9.0:1
1275 cc	9.75:1
Bmep: 970 cc	142 lb/in^2 (9.98 kg/cm^2) at 4,500 rev/min
1071 cc	143 lb/in^2 (10.05 kg/cm^2) at 4,500 rev/min
1275 cc	153 lb/in^2 (10.76 kg/cm^2) at 3,000 rev/min
Torque: 970 cc	57 lb ft (7.88 kg m) at 5,000 rev/min
1071 cc	62 lb ft (8.58 kg m) at 4,500 rev/min
1275 cc	79 lb ft (10.92 kg m) at 3,000 rev/min

Mini 1275 GT

Type	12H
Bore	2.78 in. (70.61 mm)
Stroke	3.2 in. (81.28 mm)
Capacity	77.8 in^3 (1274.8 cm^3)
Compression ratio:	
High compression	8.8:1
Low compression	8.3:1
Bmep	130 lb/in^2 (9.14 kg/cm^2) at 2,500 rev/min
Torque	84 lb ft (9.2 kg m) at 2,500 rev/min

Mini Clubman 1100

Type	10H
Bore	2.543 in. (64.588 mm)
Stroke	3.296 in. (83.73 mm)
Capacity	66.96 in^3 (1098 cc)
Compression ratio	8.5:1
Bmep	127 lb/in^2 (8.85 kg/cm^2) at 2,700 rev/min
Torque	56 lb ft (7.7 kg m) at 2,700 rev/min

Cumulative Mini production figures since inception, August 1959, to end of 1988

	850/1000 saloons	Clubman/ saloon	Wolseley Hornet	Riley Elf	Mini Estate	Clubman Estate
Home sales	1,285,018	168,279	27,358	27,690	151,775	144,318
Export sales	1,738,724	163,396	1097	3222	62,768	32,370
Total UK	3,023,742	331,675	28,455	30,912	214,543	176,688
% exported	57.5	49.3	3.9	10.4	29.2	18.3
Overseas production	385,205					
Total production	3,408,947	331,675	28,455	30,912	214,543	176,688

	Mini Cooper	Mini Cooper S	Mini 1275GT	Mini 1300*	Mini Van	Mini Pick-up	Mini Moke
Home sales	33,430	9467	34,717		416,503	43,530	1467
Export sales	66,621	35,392	81,771	21,360	84,748	14,649	13,051
Total UK	100,051	44,859	116,448	21,360	501,251	58,179	14,518
% exported	66.6	78.9	70.7	100	16.9	25.2	89.9
Overseas production		583	1,461		20,243		22,507
Total production	100,051	45,442	17,949	21,360	521,494	58,179	34,025

*Mini 1300 not sold in the UK

Production of range to end of 1988.
Vans, pick-ups, estates and mokes discontinued end 1982

	Saloons and Estates (all)	Vans and Pick-ups (all)	Mokes	Grand Totals
Home sales	1,891,292	460,033	1,467	2,352,792
Export sales	2,210,429	99,397	13,051	2,322,877
Total UK	4,101,721	559,430	14,518	4,675,669
% exported	54.0	17.8	89.9	49.6
Overseas production	387,249	20,243	22,507	429,999
Total production	4,488,970	579,673	37,025	5,105,668

Total Mini production, world-wide.

1959	19,749		1974	255,336	
1960	116,677		1975	200,293	
1961	157,059		1976	203,575	4 million
1962	216,087		1977	214,134	
1963	236,713		1978	196,799	
1964	244,359		1979	165,502	
1965	221,974	1 million	1980	150,067	
1966	213,694		1981	69,986	
1967	237,227		1982	56,297	
1968	246,066		1983	49,956	
1969	254,957	2 million	1984	35,036	
1970	278,950		1985	34,974	
1971	318,475		1986	33,740	5 million
1972	306,937	3 million	1987	32,717	
1973	295,186		1988(E)	31,979	

UK sales to end October 1988
City, Mayfair and Limited Editions.

Mayfair	46,065	Jet Black	1,528
Mayfair Auto	7,694	Red Hot	1,024
City	44,995	Advantage	2,992
City Auto	3,803	Park Lane	1,495
Mini 25	3,511	Piccadilly	2,484
Mini Sprite	2,475	Chelsea	1,465
Designer	1,755	Ritz	2,061

Mini Exports—Major Markets 1980–1988.

	1980	1981	1982	1983	1984	1985	1986	1987	1–10 1988
Belgium	2,468	1,745	2,098	2,069	1,625	1,357	978	797	541
France	14,290	9,342	8,411	7,512	6,861	6,443	6,719	8,140	6,371
Germany	2,291	1,177	503	1,130	2,988	2,613	4,578	3,612	2,702
Ireland	2,916	1,632	862	681	629	170	122	105	82
Italy	5,343	5,525	2,758	2,724	2,053	1,431	1,092	963	1,010
Netherlands	2,820	1,290	1,313	3,373	1,704	1,503	1,531	1,434	1,924
Portugal	2,110	1,910	1,628	334	543	144	131		
Japan	201	607	1,190	980	821	1,038	2,280	3,884	4,518
S.A.	2,785	2,829	3,382	2,322	312				
N-Z	1,298	651	409						
Taiwan					5	144	87	250	377
Total	46,593	31,817	23,819	21,613	18,005	15,465	18,202	20,190	18,021

Index